West Africa

New and Future Titles in the Indigenous Peoples of Africa Series Include:

West Africa
East Africa

West Africa

Tony Zurlo

Lucent Books, Inc.

P.O. Box 289011, San Diego, California

On cover: Three Masai Warriors.

Library of Congress Cataloging-in-Publication Data

Zurlo, Tony.
    West Africa / by Tony Zurlo.
      p.   cm. — (Indigenous peoples of Africa)
    Includes bibliographical references (p.).
    Summary: Discusses the history, geography, and climate of West
Africa, including ancient kingdoms, colonialism, independence, religion,
arts, the family, and the community.
    ISBN 1-56006-832-9
    1. Ethnology—Africa, West—Juvenile literature. 2. Indigenous peo-
ples—Africa, West —Juvenile literature. 3. Africa, West—Social life and
customs—Juvenile literature. [1. Ethnology—Africa, West. 2. Indigenous
Peoples—Africa, West. 3. Africa, West.] I. Title. II. Series.
  GN652.5 .Z87 2002
  305.8'00966—dc21

                                                              00-011-84

Contents

Foreword

Long recognized as the birthplace of humankind, the continent of Africa has, for centuries, been inhabited by a diverse population. Physically separated by deserts, valleys, and lush forests, the people of Africa succeeded in creating unique cultural identities and lifestyles that perfectly suited the lands on which they lived. The Masai of East Africa's Great Rift Valley, for instance, became skilled plains warriors, able to hunt food and protect their communities on an open landscape. And the Ibo of Nigeria adapted their clothing and shelter-building techniques to suit life in a tropical climate.

These isolated cultures collided with outside influences during the fifteenth century as Arab and European traders landed on African shores and ventured inland. The traders came to Africa in search of valuables: gold, ivory, and diamonds. They found these items and more. One of the continent's most profitable resources turned out to be the Africans themselves. The traders ultimately conquered and enslaved entire tribes and villages. Thus began the international slave trade, which dispersed the Africans to countries around the world.

During the five centuries that followed, Africa's population was indelibly influ-enced by the traders and their descendents. Islam and Christianity, religions of the Arabs and Europeans, merged with traditional African beliefs. Furthermore, the power and influence of the traders—the Europeans in particular—supplanted local tribal law and led to hundreds of years of imperial rule. Yet, in spite of these influences and changes, the people of Africa managed to sustain their individual cultures and ways of life. Languages, rites of passage, tribal legends–all remained unique to the tribes that practiced them.

The *Indigenous Peoples of Africa* series examines that diversity by presenting a complex and realistic picture of the various tribal cultures. Each book in the series offers historical perspectives as well as a view of contemporary life in all of the continent's regions. The series examines family life, spirituality, art, interaction with outsiders, work, education, and the challenges faced by Africa's population today.

In many cases, those challenges are daunting. AIDS and other infectious diseases wipe out entire villages. Many African children never attend school. Human rights violations abound. Refugees of tribal warfare starve in substandard camps. Government censorship prevents citizens and journalists from speaking out against corrupt political leaders. However, even on this continent devastated by famine, ravaged by disease, and torn by war, the African people endure, bound by tradition and guided by history.

Africans also catch glimpses of a bright future. In western Africa, twenty-first century political leaders are endorsing democratic forms of government. In Kenya, a mobile library brings books to people living in isolated rural regions. And in Ethiopia, the current government sponsors training programs aimed at teaching the local population farming and agricultural techniques.

The Indigenous Peoples of Africa series attempts to capture both the Africans' history and their future, their rich culture and their current challenges. Fully documented primary and secondary source quotations enliven the text. Sidebars highlight events, personalities, and traditions. Bibliographies provide readers with ideas for further research. Each book in this dynamic series provides students with a wealth of information as well as launching points for further research.

Diverse Lands, Diverse Peoples

The term *West Africa* refers to the landmass between the southern edge of the Sahara Desert and the Atlantic Ocean. Shaped somewhat like the United States, its widest portion stretches twenty-five hundred miles from the mouth of the Senegal River eastward to Lake Chad. Beginning with Nigeria, located in the far southeastern portion of this region, the countries situated along the Atlantic coastline include Benin, Togo, Ghana, Ivory Coast, Liberia, Sierra Leone, Guinea, Guinea-Bissau, Senegal, Gambia, Mauritania, and Cape Verde (an island nation). The other West African nations are landlocked. These include, east to west, Niger (located on the northern border of Nigeria), Burkina Faso, and Mali.

With 250 million people and one of the highest population growth rates in the world, West Africa will likely pass the U.S. population by midcentury. Although population figures vary as much as 10 to 15 percent depending on the source, almost half of the people of West Africa,

120 million, live in Nigeria. Ghana is the second largest, but it only has 20 million, one-tenth of Nigeria's population. The third-largest nation is Ivory Coast, with 16 million. Mali, Burkina Faso, Niger, and Senegal are home to between 10 and 11 million each.

Ethnic Groups and Native Languages

Close to 900 different ethnic groups live in West Africa. Nigeria alone is home to approximately 250 groups. As a result, people identify themselves not just as citizens of a single nation but also as members of a specific ethnic group.

These groups are classified by their native language; therefore, people who speak Hausa as their primary language are normally classified as Hausa by their national government. Over generations, people speaking the same language develop their own distinct customs, giving them even more distinguishing characteristics from neighboring ethnic groups. As a result, the

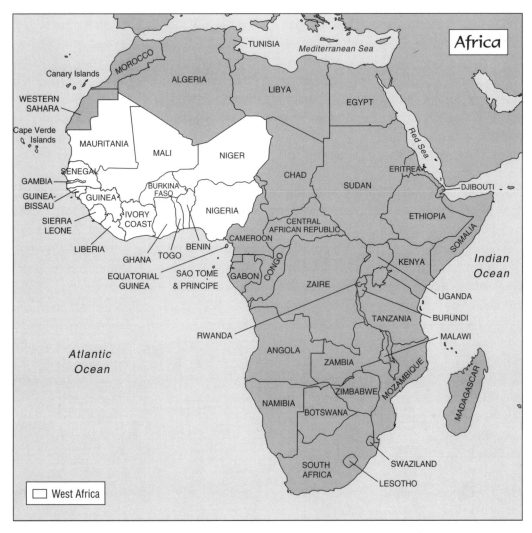

overwhelming majority of these groups number fewer than 4 million people each. For example, the Mossi of Burkina Faso, Wolof of Senegal, Baoule of Ivory Coast, Peuhl of Guinea and Mali, and Bambara of Mali each number between 3 and 4 million. The Tenne and Mende of Sierra Leone number a little over 1 million people each. The Dogon of Mali are fewer than 500,000.

Nigeria contains the three largest ethnic groups in West Africa: the Hausa/Fulani, over 40 million; the Yoruba, 30 million; and the Ibo, about 15 million. When the Akan in Ghana and the Mande of the western Sudan are added in, these five ethnic groups alone combine to make up more than 40 percent of the people of West Africa.

So many languages are spoken even in the same nations that often people cannot understand someone from a different part of the country. In a country the size of Nigeria, with over 250 different ethnic groups speaking different languages, miscommunications can lead to civil disorder. The language hurdle exists in all West African nations. Ghana has 75 different ethnic groups, and Ivory Coast has 60. Even in a small nation like Liberia, with only 3 million people, there are more than 15 different ethnic groups, each of whom speak different languages.

Throughout West Africa, the problem of multiple languages led national governments to adopt a single language for education and government business. They adopted the language of their former colonial ruler, so Gambia, Ghana, Nigeria, and Sierra Leone use English; Benin, Burkina Faso, Guinea, Ivory Coast, Mali, Togo, and Senegal use French; Cape Verde and Guinea-Bissau use Portuguese. Liberia was founded by American free blacks, so it has always used English as its official language. Only Mauritania, ruled by France, has gone to a different language. After many centuries of mixing with North Africa, Mauritania adopted Arabic as its official language.

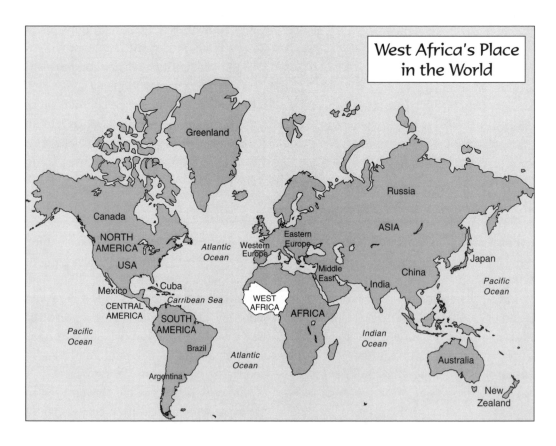

West Africa's Place in the World

Life in West Africa

Even with the great variety of languages, people across the region have many features in common. From the edges of the Sahara Desert to the Atlantic coast, all ethnic groups emphasize the values of the extended family and community over individualism. Even their traditional religious views are similar, with a belief in a single creator, a spirit world, and the influence of ancestors who live in the spirit world. For all West Africans, daily living is connected in some way to their traditional religious ideas.

Although there is no absolute proof, many of the people in the coastal and forest sections of West Africa probably migrated from the central part of the continent, through modern-day Nigeria, Benin, Togo, Ghana, and up the Atlantic coast. They rarely migrated north of the forest belt. North of the forests, however, where the geography shifts to a dry, arid climate, the ethnic groups had ties to the north, across the Sahara Desert. People in the western Sudan have a shared history in the early kingdoms of Ghana, Mali, and Songhai. From their North African ties, the majority of people in the western Sudan also converted to Islam over the centuries.

Today the people of this region face huge challenges as they try to catch up economically with the more developed nations of the world. Individually, many of the countries in West Africa have too few resources to make much progress. Collectively, however, the region has enough diversity of land and resources to enable its people to someday compete successfully with the rest of the world.

The solutions to many of the problems throughout the region require building new industries, expanding highways and transportation systems, and improving the health and nutrition of the local people. To do this, however, these nations will have to overcome internal ethnic conflicts so that their people can move forward as a unified force of progress. These are the challenges that face West African countries as they enter the twenty-first century.

Chapter 1

Geography and Climate

Two major geographic features dominate life in West Africa: water and sand. The moisture from the Atlantic Ocean progresses inland for hundreds of miles until it reaches hot, dry air blowing southward from the Sahara Desert. The area where these climatic forces meet, along the twelfth parallel of north latitude, divides the northern part, referred to as the Sudan—a word adapted from the Arabic *Bilad as-Sudan* meaning "Land of the Negroes"—from the south. The rain forest and coastal lands are called Guinea, a word derived from the North African Berber phrase *Akal n-Iguinawen*, meaning "Black Man."

The Coastal Lands

Mangrove swamps and tropical rain forests, dotted occasionally with clusters of islands such as the Bunce and Sherbro Islands off of Sierra Leone, make up West Africa's coastal area. The swamplands are thick with bamboo forests, raffia palms, vines, mangrove trees, and creepers. In most areas, within fifty miles of the coastal swamp-

The coastal region of West Africa is a land of lush rain forests.

lands, the rain forests begin, with iroko, ebony, mahogany, and other hardwood trees towering two hundred feet into the sky, shading the land from direct sunlight.

People living in this part of West Africa must adapt to year-round humidity of over 80 percent and 70 to 90 degree Fahrenheit temperatures. Although rainfall varies, some areas in the Niger Delta of Nigeria receive more than 144 inches a year. Two capital cities, Monrovia, Liberia, and Freetown, Sierra Leone, average close to 80 inches during the peak rainy season months of June and July alone. Another round of heavy rain hits the coastal area in September and October.

A thousand years ago, the rain forests prevented large settlements of people. Once iron tools were introduced, however, the forestlands could be cleared for cultivation. Imported crops that could grow in intense heat and shade ensured that people could survive. Eventually they congregated in small cleared-out patches in the rain forests from Nigeria through Togo and from western Ghana to Sierra Leone. Palm oil and kola nuts, along with plantains and a variety of tubers such as cassava and yams, grew abundantly in this area. But the tropical forestland remained a dividing line between the people of the coast and those living farther north in the western Sudan.

The Guinea forestland is home to one of West Africa's largest ethnic groups, the Yoruba, who number more than 30 million today. The majority of the people live in cities, often combining small farming with other occupations. For several cen-

The Kola Nut

The kola nut, which measures about two inches long, is cultivated from a sixty-foot evergreen tree and is dried in the sun before it is collected and distributed for the market. The nut's bitter taste makes it unpopular with many foreign visitors to West Africa. However, no respectable African host would receive a guest without offering to "break kola." Historian E. W. Bovill, in his book *The Golden Trade of the Moors*, describes the nut's significance.

"The twin interlocking kernels were regarded as a symbol of friendship, and no present was complete without kolas. The nut consequently acquired a ceremonial importance, and it became customary to swear oaths on a kola. Its bitter flavour appeals strongly to the African, it is undoubtedly very sustaining and it is widely regarded as a cure for impotency."

turies their cities have been a crossroads for trade with both the western Sudan to the north and the Guinea coast to the south. Because of this extensive contact with other people, the Yoruba developed sophisticated political skills. Much of the leadership for Nigeria's independence in the 1940s and 1950s came from Yoruba leaders such as Obafemi Awolowo and S. L. Akintola. The Yoruba also excel in the arts, especially bronze and wood sculpture, music, and drama.

Another major ethnic group in the southern part of West Africa is the Akan in Ghana, numbering between 8 and 9 million people, the Akan include two major subgroups: the Ashanti and the Fanti. During the mid–seventeenth century the Ashanti developed a powerful kingdom that controlled much of modern-day Ghana for 150 years. The Ashanti trace their descent through the female side of the family, rather than the male's side. Therefore, a husband considers his sisters, his mother, and his mother's relations as his immediate relatives. His wife, likewise, looks to her mother and sisters as her immediate relatives.

Western Sudan

The rain forest varies from fifty to a hundred miles deep. From there, the land rises

A Yoruba Elder. The Yoruba are one of the major ethnic groups in West Africa.

slowly and opens into vast rolling hills and grasslands called savanna, approximately a thousand feet above sea level. The savanna extends northward in most places for two to three hundred miles. The only place that the savanna breaks through to the Atlantic Ocean is between the Pra River in eastern Ghana and the Yewa River in western Nigeria, covering the nations of Togo and Benin. As people continue to level rain forests for lumber and cultivation, however, the savanna edges southward closer to the coast in other parts of West Africa.

Life in the savanna grasslands can be pleasant, as long as the rains are consistent. In a normal year, the savanna can get as much as forty inches of rain. The rains come in one distinct season, beginning in May and ending in late September or October.

A major cause of this seasonal cycle is the Harmattan, a wind blowing south from the Sahara Desert that dries out the air between November and April. Often, the sand carried by the winds dims the sunlight. As a result, a dull tan haze hangs in the sky until the first rains appear again in the spring with the humid air advancing northward from the ocean. Because of the mild climate, the most popular crops are millet, sorghum, and peanuts.

The largest ethnic group in the western Sudan is the Hausa. Numbering at least 23 million, the Hausa form the majority population of northern Nigeria and Niger. Their language has become the lingua franca, or common language, of the people throughout this part of Africa, and it is the primary language for close to 50 million people in West Africa.

Another ethnic group, the Fulani, have intermarried with the Hausa, so today ethnologists sometimes combine the two in censuses. Combined, the Hausa and the Fulani number between 40 and 50 million. Mostly farmers, the Hausa are also famed for their leatherwork, textiles, and other crafts. Many thousands are also traders who can be found in all the major cities of West Africa. Almost all practice the Muslim religion.

Sahel and Sahara

The savanna changes into the Sahel, a semiarid belt of mostly scrub bushes and flat-top acacia trees. The Sahel is more than two hundred miles wide in some parts of West Africa. It is difficult to determine exactly where the Sahel ends and the Sahara Desert begins. Much of northern Nigeria and Burkina Faso are in the Sahel, but the countries of Mauritania, Mali, and Niger are mostly desert.

Less than ten inches of rain falls annually throughout most of the area. Some locations might not see rain for half a year until the next rainy season. Even along the Atlantic Ocean in Mauritania, the capital, Nouakchott, receives only about ten inches of rain annually, and over half of that comes in August.

The arid heat and sparse rainfall cause frequent crop failures, so life in this area is difficult. For this reason, the majority of people tend to live along riverbanks in the Sahel. The capital cities of Mali (Bamako)

The Baobab Tree

One West African legend says that a god became angry with the baobab tree and yanked it from the ground. Then the god jammed it back into the ground upside down. The tree is famous for its thick trunk and branches that look like an extensive web of roots growing toward the sky.

West Africans think highly of the baobab tree because of its many uses. Thriving in the semiarid western Sudan, the baobab trunk is almost hollow, so rainwater sometimes accumulates inside. Its large pods, called "monkey bread," are made into cups and bowls. Sometimes the pods are used as cooking fuel as well. The people eat the seeds or make a drink from them. They also chop and boil the leaves to make a sauce. When the leaves are dried and ground into a paste, the people use it as medication for skin sores and joint problems.

Baobab trees such as this one provide valuable raw materials for the people of western Sudan.

A nomad and his camel in the Sahel, which lies between the savanna and the Sahara Desert.

and Niger (Niamey) are both along the Niger River. These parts of the Sahel receive up to forty inches of rain a year between May and October.

This area is the home of the Mande ethnic group, which formed the core of the great kingdoms of the western Sudan between A.D. 1000 and 1700. Today the majority of Mande are Muslim, although many still follow some of their ancient religious traditions, such as paying tribute to ancestors. The Mande include the Mandinka, Malinke, Dyula, Marka, Mende, Bambara, and Soninke subgroups. Numbering at least 10 million today, they live mainly in Senegal, Mali, Guinea, Sierra Leone, and Liberia. Although they practice crafts and trades, most Mande are farmers.

Rivers

Because of West Africa's hot climate, rivers play a significant role in the lives of the people. Extending across West Africa for 2,590 miles, the Niger River is longer than the Mississippi and is the third-longest river in Africa. It originates 310 miles from the

Atlantic Ocean in the highlands of Guinea. Flowing northeastward toward the Sahara Desert, the Niger River reaches its northernmost point in Mali, near the fabled city of Timbuktu (also known as Tombouctou).

From Timbuktu, the Niger River winds southeast through the western edge of the Republic of Niger and divides the southwestern part of Nigeria from the northern. People in this region are able to farm and conduct trade along the Niger River, which cuts through the southern portions of Mali, Burkina Faso, and Niger before it turns southward toward the Atlantic Ocean.

The Niger River joins with another large river, the Benue, in the center of Nigeria. From there, the Niger River turns southward until it spreads out into an enormous web of swamps and creeks called the Niger Delta, about 140 miles from the Atlantic Ocean. The delta, covering 120 miles of coastline, has become the center of one of the world's largest oil-drilling industries.

The other rivers of West Africa are short in comparison. Located in the western portion of West Africa, the Senegal River begins in the highlands of Guinea. From there, it winds one thousand miles westward, forming the border between Mauritania and Senegal and emptying into the Atlantic Ocean. Along its banks can be found the Djoudj National Park, famous for its large flocks of flamingos and pelicans.

Another major river in far West Africa is the Gambia. Beginning in the highlands of Guinea, it flows west 620 miles through the center of Senegal. Along the river's shoreline the tiny nation of Gambia was created, 186 miles long and an average of 22 miles wide. The Gambian people rely almost completely on this river for economic survival. The river is famous for its bird sanctuaries, with over 560 different species identified.

From Guinea to Ghana, many smaller rivers flow into the lagoons and swamplands of West Africa. In eastern Ghana, the Volta River system runs out of the highlands of Burkina Faso for 1,000 miles southward into the Atlantic Ocean. About 100 miles inland, the Ghanaian government built the 196-feet-high Volta Dam, creating one of the world's largest artificial lakes, covering a 3,275-square-mile area in northeast and central Ghana. It provides extensive hydroelectric power, irrigation, and other benefits for the country.

Mountains

In this vast region, mountains are rare. The highest ones in West Africa lie along Nigeria's border with Cameroon. Cappal Wadi, the tallest peak in West Africa, is only 7,931 feet high. The next highest mountains are the 6,632-feet-high Aïr Massif in northern Niger. These mountains, rising in the middle of the desert, take up an area the size of Switzerland and are home to animals, such as goats, camels, and antelopes, as well as a variety of trees and plant life.

In Sierra Leone, Mount Bintumani rises 6,370 feet just off the coastline, the only part of West Africa's coastline where mountains begin near the sea. The other major mountain area is along the border

The Niger River is the longest of the waterways in West Africa and the third largest river in all of Africa.

shared by Guinea, Ivory Coast, and Liberia, where the highest point is Mount Nimba at 5,747 feet. The Fouta Djallon highlands, rising to 4,920 feet in western Guinea, is the source of several rivers, including the Senegal, Gambia, and part of the Niger.

Paths of Settlement

The natural climate and land division led the West African people to take two divergent paths in settlement. Because of the thick forests, the people living south of the savanna developed small, self-sufficient villages and towns. The only forest kingdoms that expanded to any extent before the European contact in the sixteenth century lived on the fringes of the savanna.

Kingdoms extending outward from the towns of Oyo and Benin (in modern-day Nigeria), for example, controlled territory of a few hundred square miles prior to the rise of the slave trade.

People north of the rain forests live in an area with wide plains and an environment allowing the use of camels and horses for transportation. The various ethnic groups in the western Sudan traded and intermarried with each other and built large cities, some of which grew into large feudal empires such as Ghana, Mali, and Songhai. Throughout history, they exchanged goods and ideas with North Africa and the Middle East rather than with the lands to the south.

Chapter 2

Kingdoms of the Western Sudan

West Africans in the western Sudan have had a long history of contact with North Africa, especially after the introduction of the camel around A.D. 300. At the time, Africa was the major supplier of gold to North Africa, southern Europe, and the Middle East. By the year 1000, huge caravans of traders with several hundred camels were crossing the Sahara carrying beads, silks, and other manufactured goods from the Mediterranean coast. These North African traders also brought with them the religious ideas of Muhammad, the founder of Islam, a religion that centuries later would become the common religion of nearly all of the people of the western Sudan.

Between 1000 and 1700, the African kingdoms of Ghana, Mali, and Songhai succeeded each other as the supreme power in the region. These kingdoms controlled an area extending a thousand miles north from the edge of the forest in present-day Ghana to the southern tip of Algeria and another thousand miles east from the Senegal River across the Sahel and southern Sahara into modern-day northern Nigeria.

Their reputations hinged on controlling the Saharan trade and its profits from gold and salt. As long as the defeated states paid tribute in crops, cloth, gold, or other products, the controlling power rarely interfered with the political or religious customs of the people.

Sahara Caravans and West African Kingdoms

For over a thousand years, traders inched their way across the Sahara with their camel trains. Their first stop was the Taghaza salt mines (in modern-day southern Morocco). After loading up with salt, they set out on the two-month trek through the desert to Timbuktu. Traders from towns south of the Niger River brought gold, kola nuts, hides, and other goods to exchange with North African traders.

The trek between Morocco and Timbuktu followed ancient trails known only to the Tuaregs, a group of desert nomads who served as guides. The caravans covered about three miles in the morning before stopping in the scorching heat, which sometimes soared above 130 degrees Fahrenheit during midday. Danger loomed everywhere, from shifting sand dunes to raids by nomadic thieves. Dried-up wells, snakes, and contaminated water were constant worries. But the trade thrived for many centuries, bringing to the western Sudan a constant influx of new people, products, and ideas. Besides Timbuktu, cities such as Djenné, Gao, Agadez, and Kano joined in the prosperity from the Saharan trade.

For centuries Timbuktu, a city in western Sudan, was a trading hub for caravans from North Africa, and for traders who traveled up the Niger River.

The Kingdom of Ghana

The first major kingdom in the western Sudan was called Ghana, after its king's title, which meant "war chief." Its influence derived from what seemed to ancient traders an endless supply of gold. Made up of the Soninke ethnic group, a Mande-speaking people, the kingdom covered an area west of Timbuktu that extended into southern modern-day Mauritania.

During the fourteenth century an Arab author living in Timbuktu wrote that in a previous century, the king's one thousand horses had "slept only on a carpet, with a silken rope for halter." He added that the king "fed as many as ten thousand subjects at one banquet."[1] For about five hundred years, the gold trade was carried out by the "silent barter" system. From Ghana's capital city of Kumbi (west of Timbuktu), North African traders would travel with Ghanaian agents southwestward to the Senegal River for twenty days. In his

21

Timbuktu

The history of Timbuktu (which is also called Tombouctou) is shrouded in mystery. One legend claims that around A.D. 1100, some Tuareg nomads put an old woman named Bouctou (meaning "Large Navel") in charge of the town, which had a water well (the word *tim* means "water well"). By the early fourteenth century, it had become an important stop on the trans-Saharan trade route. Gold dust, kola nuts, grains, and other articles were brought up the Niger River into Timbuktu to exchange for salt and dates and other supplies from the north. An active market for food, wood, cotton, silver, copper, leather, and many other goods, Timbuktu had also become a major center for Islamic scholarship. Sankore Mosque, with its Islamic scholars and students, was one of the world's best-known centers of learning at the time.

When the Sahara trade began to weaken in the seventeenth century, Timbuktu's fortunes declined. From a peak population of about two hundred thousand in the 1500s, the city only has about fifteen thousand today. The salt trade still passes through Timbuktu during the "cool" months, from October through March; but it is only a shadow of the great centuries of the past.

book *The Golden Trade of the Moors*, historian E. W. Bovill explains the process once the traders reached the river:

> Merchants beat great drums to summon the local natives, who were naked and lived in holes in the ground. From these holes, which were doubtless the pits from which they dug the gold, they refused to emerge in the presence of the foreign merchants. The latter . . . [would] arrange their trade goods in piles on the river bank and retire out of sight. The local natives then came and placed a heap of gold beside each pile and withdrew. If the merchants were satisfied they took the gold and retreated, beating their drums to signify that the market was over.[2]

Continual invasions from the Almoravids, a militant group of North African Muslims, weakened Ghana's hold on the trade. During the thirteenth century several small ethnic groups had severed Ghana's influence and were jockeying for control of the Saharan trade.

The Mali Empire

For a while the Fulani from the Senegal River area were the most powerful group to challenge Ghana. Sumanguru, the Fulani warrior-king, overwhelmed all rivals and proclaimed himself emperor of Ghana. True to his tyrannical reputation, Sumanguru tried to secure his power by killing eleven sons of his chief rival, members of the royal family of the Mandinka, also a Mande-speaking people. He spared the twelfth, Sogolon-Djata Keita, a young boy who could not even walk, thinking the boy was too sickly to be a threat. With the help of braces, Sogolon-Djata grew up to become a vigorous defender of his Mandinka heritage, taking the name Sundiata, which means "the Hungering Lion."

Sundiata conducted guerrilla warfare until 1234, when he routed Sumanguru in a legendary battle still narrated by griots (oral historian-musicians) and taught in schools throughout West Africa. Sundiata's empire was called Mali, which means "Where the King Resides." Authors Patri-

cia and Fredrick McKissack call Sundiata "the King Arthur and George Washington of Mali."[3]

Sundiata's grandson, Mansa Mūsā, or King Mūsā, became the most celebrated Mandinka ruler. When he took over in 1312, Mali's empire was one of the largest in the world. Its boundaries included the famous trading centers of Djenné, Timbuktu, and Gao, and it extended west to the coast of present-day Mauritania.

A fervent believer in Islam, Mansa Mūsā's pilgrimage to Mecca, Islam's holy city, is one of the legendary events in

The City of Mecca today. Mali ruler Mansa Mūsā's fourteenth-century pilgrimage to Mecca was so grand that it became legendary.

Sundiata Keita

In 1234 Sundiata routed Sumanguru in a legendary battle still retold by griots (storytellers) and taught in schools. The two warriors advanced with their armies toward each other. In his book *A History of West Africa*, historian Basil Davidson continues the story, according to the legend.

"When Sundiata turned his eyes on the army of Sumanguru, he believed they were a cloud and . . . said: 'What is this cloud on the eastern side?' They told him it was the army of Sumanguru. . . . When he [Sumanguru] saw the army of Sundiata, he exclaimed: 'What is that mountain of stone?' For he thought it was a mountain. And they told him: 'It is the army of Sundiata.' . . .

Then the two columns . . . fought a terrible battle. In the thick of the fight, Sundiata uttered a great shout in the face of the warriors of Sumanguru, and at once these ran to get behind Sumanguru. The latter, in his turn, uttered a great shout in the face of the warriors of Sundiata, all of whom fled to get behind Sundiata. Usually, when Sumanguru shouted, eight heads would rise above his own head. . . .

Sumanguru's witchcraft . . . proved less powerful than the witchcraft of Sundiata. . . . Sumanguru was struck with an arrow bearing the spur of a white cock, fatal to his power, and [as the famous legend concludes] 'Sumanguru vanished and was seen no more.'"

African history. He took with him thousands of people, from soldiers and servants to camel drivers and cooks. Historians record that he gave away so much gold to the people of Egypt that it took twelve years for gold to regain its former value.

Mansa Mūsā's successors were too weak to survive a barrage of attacks on the kingdom. The Tuaregs sacked Timbuktu, and the Mossi ethnic group, located south of the Niger River, rose in rebellion. But the most serious opposition came from the Songhai people in the city of Gao on the Niger River, a couple of hundred miles east of Timbuktu.

Songhai and the Rise of Sunni Ali

The Songhai had long resisted outside invaders. They declared independence from Mali after Mansa Mūsā's death. By the mid-fifteenth century, the city of Gao was powerful enough to compete for control of the Saharan trade. Its king, Sunni Ali Ber, knew he had to subdue Timbuktu and Djenné, the two major trade centers along the Niger River.

Timbuktu was controlled at the time by a corrupt non-Muslim Berber who lived with the nomads on the outskirts of the city. A few years earlier, the Muslim leaders had mocked Sunni Ali's attempt to bring Timbuktu under Songhai control. Now, however, the Muslims were so desperate that they secretly invited Sunni Ali to come liberate the city from the Berbers. He accepted.

In their book *Great Rulers of the African Past*, Lavinia Dobler and William A. Brown describe Sunni Ali's professional army as a "strong force, composed of noble cavalrymen, nomad camel drivers and captive foot soldiers. . . . These men were trained for war. The horsemen were equipped with sabers, lances, javelins, and breastplates. The foot soldiers had bows and poisoned arrows."[4] Thousands fled Timbuktu as Sunni Ali entered unopposed. Then he turned on the Muslims, killing hundreds whom he considered cowards and traitors.

Next, Sunni Ali attacked the important trading center of Djenné, only to be repelled. Unable to defeat Djenné's forces for seven years, he managed to seal off the city from outside contact, cutting off its supplies. Finally, fearing Sunni Ali's reputation for cruelty, the young Djenné king decided the city would survive only if he surrendered. Impressed with the young king's humility when they met, Sunni Ali allowed him to remain in charge of Djenné. Sunni Ali returned to his hometown and became king of Mali.

Songhai grew even stronger under another king, who, unlike his predecessors, carried the religion everywhere he went. Askia Muhammad Toure, a Soninke captured as a boy and raised as a Songhai, became one of Sunni Ali's loyal generals. When Sunni Ali died, his son took the throne and increased the persecution of Muslims. Eventually, Askia Muhammad joined a conspiracy that drove Sunni Ali's son out of Gao. Known throughout the western Sudan as Askia the Great, he ruled Songhai from 1493 to 1528. All of his appointments were devout Muslims, laying the foundation for Islamic influence throughout the region.

Leo Africanus, a Moroccan Berber traveling throughout West Africa in the early sixteenth century, was greatly impressed by the intellectual flavor of Timbuktu under Askia Muhammad. He wrote, "There

After many years of persecution, Muslims— followers of the prophet Muhammad (pictured)—gained prominence in western Sudan in the late fifteenth century.

are numerous judges, doctors, and clerics . . . all receiving good salaries from the king. He pays great respect to men of learning. . . . [Books] are sold for more money than any other merchandise."[5]

Leo Africanus described Djenné as "a city prospering from its crops of rice, barley, fish, cattle and cotton. The cotton is a major crop sold unto the merchants of Barbary for cloth of Europe, for brass vessels, for armor and such other commodities."[6] Much more than Timbuktu, Djenné represented genuinely West African greatness in Islamic scholarship.

Askia Muhammad took control of the Taghaza salt mines and Agadez (in northern Niger), and he defeated the major Hausa city-states, including Kano, Katsina, and Zaria. He maintained power by his skillful political organization. Each clan, or group of families, was assigned specific duties. One sent men and women to serve Askia Muhammad at his court. Others had to make weapons and ironwork. He also appointed ministers to head various government departments, such as the navy, army, fishing, and tax collecting.

The Decline of Songhai

After Askia Muhammad's death, the Songhai kings successfully defended the empire for a few decades, but the pendulum of history was about to swing. Moroccan Berbers coveted the salt mines under Songhai's control. By 1600 a revolutionary change in warfare—an early version of the musket—enabled a Moroccan army to overrun the major Songhai cities. Just as important, however, in the decline of Songhai was the rise of European contact along the West African coast. Europeans, formerly dependent on the Saharan trade for gold, ivory, and other goods, now began trading for these at ports controlled by Africans from modern-day Senegal to Nigeria. As a result, the Saharan trade declined in significance. The western Sudan dissolved into many smaller rival states.

The Moroccans were interested only in controlling the trade, not in empire building. A century of disorder followed. Historian 'Abd ar-Rahmān as-Sa'dī recorded in the seventeenth century that "security has given place to danger, prosperity to misery and calamity, whilst affliction and distress have succeeded wellbeing . . . raiding and war sparing neither life nor wealth nor status, disorder spreading and intensifying until it became universal."[7]

Kanem-Bornu, located along the western shores of Lake Chad, dominated the eastern edge of the western Sudan. Ruled by the Kanuri ethnic group, Kanem-Bornu drew its trade directly from the north with Egypt and modern-day Tunisia rather than from the western Sudan kingdoms. From its beginning, the kingdom was ruled by the Sefuwa family. The leaders converted to Islam early and maintained a strong loyalty to the religion. Like the leaders of Ghana, Mali, and Songhai, the kings of Kanem-Bornu were more interested in maintaining power than in converting the land to Islam. As long as villagers paid their taxes and did not challenge the Sefuwas' right to rule, they were left alone to continue life as their ancestors had lived for centuries.

Kanem-Bornu reached its peak of influence under King Idris Alooma, who reigned from 1580 until 1617. The kingdom's army was strong enough to drive the Songhai out of what is today central Niger. At its peak, Kanem-Bornu controlled hundreds of miles of territory, east into modern-day Sudan, north to the borders of Tunisia and Libya, and west near the Hausa city-state of Kano.

Generally, the leaders of the western Sudan empires practiced Islam. Looking for qualified men to serve as government officials, the kings frequently turned to Fulani men, who tended to be well educated from years of studying the Koran, the Muslim holy book. But by the late eighteenth century, many officials had become lax in their religious practices. Some even reverted to practicing traditional African religions alongside Islam. As a result, Muslim reformers began criticizing publicly the mixing of Islam and traditional African beliefs.

Uthman dan Fodio Leads an Islamic Jihad

The best known of these reformers was the Fulani scholar and mystic Uthman dan Fodio, who hailed from a small village in the northeast corner of modern-day Nigeria. Uthman writes that when he was forty years old, he had a vision "to unsheathe the sword of truth."[8] Soon after, he called for a jihad, or religious war, to overthrow the Hausa rulers of the several independent city-states across what is today northern Nigeria. Uthman justified the war by claiming the Hausa leaders had discarded Islamic principles.

His promise of a just administration impressed the people, and the Fulani, behind Uthman's leadership, were able to defeat the Hausa states of Kano, Katsina, Zaria, and Gobir in only four years. By 1810 Uthman dan Fodio had changed the destiny of tens of millions of West Africans with his revolution. He had studied carefully the lives and works of Muhammad, the founder of Islam, and other reformers of the western Sudan, especially Askia the Great. But as historian Thomas Hodgkin writes, Uthman "also looked forward—to the new social and moral order which it [his revolution] sought to establish. . . . It was [his] social teaching—his attack upon current forms of oppression, exploitation, and injustice—that caused the *jihad*, in its initial stages, to appeal especially to the submerged classes, among the Hausa as well as among the Fulani."[9]

Uthman appointed his brother and son as governors of what is today most of northern Nigeria. His empire extended for more than four hundred miles west to east and about three hundred miles north to south. Muslim teachers spread out into all parts of the region to preach Muhammad's message. And the new leaders were honest and open in their dealings with the common people. Uthman dan Fodio's legacy remains the most powerful unifying force in northern Nigeria today.

These children are studying at a Koranic school in northern Nigeria. After a jihad (holy war) by early-nineteenth-century Islamic reformers, Muslim teachers spread Muhammad's message throughout the region.

The Heritage of the Western Sudan Empires

After 1700 European trade along the Atlantic coast, especially the slave trade, shifted West Africans' attention southward. The Europeans conducted their business with Africans along the Atlantic coast, and the value of the Saharan trade diminished.

The impact of these famous western Sudan kingdoms, however, is still felt today.

The majority of the people share a sense of pride in their collective history. The modern nations of Ghana and Mali were named after the ancient empires. The famous kings of Mali and Songhai, such as Sundiata, Mansa Mūsā, Sunni Ali Ber, and Askia Muhammad, are still heralded in stories throughout West Africa. And although Islam took several centuries to spread beyond the ruling class, today it is the dominant religion of the entire western Sudan.

Chapter 3

The Forest Kingdoms

When the great armies of Mali or Songhai tried to advance south into the forest regions of West Africa, they found the hot, wet climate and thick vegetation forbidding. There is no written record of the people who inhabited the regions, so little is known of their early civilization. During the nineteenth and twentieth centuries, archaeologists discovered ruins throughout the forest and coastal areas of several centralized states with obviously sophisticated cultures. The thick tropical rain forests protecting these societies from their northern neighbors also restricted them to much smaller sizes than the western Sudanese kingdoms. However, states such as Oyo and Benin in Nigeria, Ashanti in Ghana, and Dahomey in modern-day Benin managed to extend their authority for hundreds of miles, from the coastline to the southern edge of the savanna. Because these states had more contact with peoples of the north, more is known about them. Those that remained behind the forest curtain remained a mystery until European traders landed along the hidden coastline in the fifteenth century.

The Oyo Kingdom

The Yoruba people of the forest regions regard a legendary figure named Oduduwa as their first ancestor. From his home in the city of Ile-Ifé, his seven sons branched out and founded major towns. One son, Oranmiyan, set up his capital in Oyo. Oranmiyan's grave is still a popular shrine there.

Archaeological evidence reveals that by the year 1300 Yoruba towns were surrounded by large walls, with agricultural fields located outside the walls. They also carried on extensive trade with the Hausa and other people to the north.

Around the beginning of the fifteenth century, a young prince named Shango routed all rivals and established himself as *alafin*, or "king," of Oyo and the Yoruba people. He expanded his empire in all directions, establishing Oyo as one of the more powerful kingdoms centered just north of the Guinea forest region. Because they had access to the savanna, officials were able to tame horses and build a powerful cavalry. Taking advantage of their potent military, Oyo eventually expanded northward across the Niger River to the edges of Hausaland and westward as far as modern-day Ghana.

The *alafin* ruled with the advice of a council of state consisting of seven noblemen who actually ran the kingdom's affairs. They elected the new *alafin* from royal family candidates. An independent group of prominent freemen organized a secret society called the Ogboni. They developed into a powerful nongovernmental organization influencing the affairs of Oyo. This complex political arrangement was repeated in all Yoruba cities. As long as they paid tribute and taxes to the central government, the cities were left to run their own local affairs.

The *alafin* at Oyo was considered divine, however, so he wielded great power. Besides an enormous income from the provinces and cities, he had a court filled with officials, servants, and slaves ready to heed his command. But holding onto power involved constant fighting. Internal rebellion cast the Yoruba cities into a series of destructive civil wars. From the ashes of centuries of strife, Ibadan emerged in the 1800s as the most influential city in Yorubaland. But by then, the British had taken control of Nigeria.

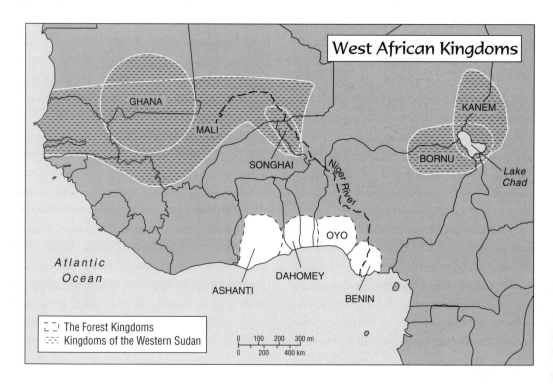

West African Kingdoms

GHANA
KANEM
MALI
SONGHAI
Niger River
BORNU
Lake Chad
OYO
Atlantic Ocean
DAHOMEY
ASHANTI
BENIN

Ľ Ľ The Forest Kingdoms
Kingdoms of the Western Sudan

0   100   200   300 mi
0   200   400 km

The Edo of Benin

Although their histories are linked, the Yoruba and Edo people are different ethnic groups. It is not clear why a Yoruba leader tried to rule the Edo of Benin around 1400. Either the Edo were dissatisfied with their own rulers and invited him, or the Oyo kingdom was expanding militarily into the area. At that time, Yoruba prince Oranmiyan arrived in Benin City and married an Edo princess. He remained only a short time, however. One report claims he decided that he did not know enough about the local customs to rule successfully. But before he returned to Ile-Ifé, he made sure his son, Eweka, would become the new king, called the *oba*, of Benin.

Under the Eweka dynasty, Benin became a major power in southern Nigeria. In the late 1400s Portugal exchanged ambassadors with Benin. The kingdom flourished, and by 1600, Benin ruled much of the southwestern and south-central portion of modern-day Nigeria. A Dutch observer at the time wrote that the people of Benin "are very conscionable, and will doe no wrong to the other, neither will take anything from strangers, for if they doe, they should afterward be put to death."[10]

Benin maintained its power for almost three centuries. Nigerian historian J. F. Ade Ajayi writes, "The great strength of Benin was in its monarchy. . . . [The *oba*] was surrounded with a great aura of mystery, fear and respect."[11] The *oba* had to try to balance the rival claims of the village leaders and his advisers, but ultimately he had godlike power to make decisions.

The qualities of the people also promoted the kingdom's success. Although keen traders, they also stuck to high personal standards in their dealings with outsiders. Dutch trader David Van Nyendael wrote in 1702 about their good nature and sharp business skills: "They are very prompt in Business, and will not suffer any of their ancient Customs to be abolish'd; . . . If we comply with them, they are very easy to deal with, and will not be wanting in any thing on their Part requisite to a good Agreement."[12]

Very few of the inhabitants were poor. For those misfortune few, the *oba* and other officials "subsist several Poor at the Place of Residence on their Charity, employing those who are fit for any work, . . . and the rest they keep for God's Sake, and to obtain the Character of being charitable; so that here are no Beggars: And this necessary Care succeeds so well, that we do not see many remarkably poor amongst them."[13]

When the British shifted their trade to palm oil in the nineteenth century, they stepped up their efforts to destroy the slave trade and abolish slavery in Nigeria itself. At this time, the *oba* of Benin controlled only the city and immediate surroundings. But to the dismay of the British, the people continued the practice of human sacrifices. After slowly overpowering the Nigerian chiefs in the Niger Delta, the British moved inland to negotiate with the *oba* of Benin. They met resistance, so they sent in troops and destroyed the city in 1897.

An Ashanti king holds court. In the seventeenth and eighteenth centuries the Ashanti unified West African states to form a vast empire.

The Ashanti

Migrating south from the western Sudan grasslands, by 1200 the Akan people had settled north of the Guinea forest area between the branches of the Volta River, about 150 miles north of the Atlantic coast. Trade routes extending from the coast northward through the forests already linked the great commercial centers of Djenné, Timbuktu, and Kano. This extensive commerce converged near the present-day city of Kumasi, located on the northern fringe of the forest belt—the source of kola nuts and gold.

An Ashanti clan named Oyoko, under the shrewd leadership of King Osei Tutu and his chief priest and adviser Okomfo Anokye, created an empire that rivaled the strength of Oyo and Benin. Around 1690 Osei Tutu and Okomfo Anokye pulled off one of the more magical feats in West African history.

To gain the loyalty of neighboring states, they summoned the leaders to Kumasi. At the gathering, amidst thunder and lightning, Okomfo Anokye announced that the supreme god, Nyame, had commanded him to unify the Ashanti people and build a great empire. Then a wooden stool decorated with gold descended from the clouds and came to rest on Osei Tutu's knees.

Interpreting this event for the chiefs, Okomfo Anokye declared that the golden stool represented the spirit of the Ashanti people. The stool, he told them, must be protected or the Ashanti would lose their power. He concluded the event by declaring Osei Tutu the first *Asantehene*, or "king of the Ashanti."

The idea of the golden stool unified the various states with a symbol representing the soul of the Ashanti. They drew up a constitution based on Akan traditions so that all of the neighboring states would feel comfortable with the laws. Once the kings of surrounding states pledged loyalty to Osei Tutu, they became members of the council of state advising the *Asantehene*.

In 1701 the Ashanti army under Osei Tutu took control of the town of Elmina and its notorious fort on the coast which was rented by the Dutch to house slaves waiting to board ships. For almost two centuries, the Ashanti controlled the affairs of this entire area. During the nineteenth century the British fought a series of battles to

Ashanti Stools

The symbol of authority in Ashanti society is a carved stool. But nowadays everyone owns a carved stool. Fathers give carved stools as their first present to sons; men give stools to their fiancées. Stools are carved with elaborate designs, which become more detailed and decorative the higher the person's status. The golden stool of the king of the Ashanti is the most elaborately decorated.

African art specialist Michael Conner explains the care given to stools in his essay "Welcome to Cutting to the Essence, Shaping for the Fire."

"[The artists] carve stools in soft, white wood. They are kept white by regular washing. Gradually, vigorous scrubbing and constant use wear down the surface and necessitate repairs. After the owner dies, however, his favorite stool would be ritually blackened, ornamented with charms, and transformed into a religious icon through which the living can communicate with their lineage of ancestors."

The British took control of the Ashanti empire in 1896. Here, Ashanti royalty are depicted in submission to British officers.

subdue the Ashanti and finally overthrew the king in 1896.

The longevity of the Ashanti union can be traced to the sophisticated mix of ritual and shrewd administrative appointments by Osei Tutu and Okomfo Anokye. In some cases, defeated rulers were appointed to major positions in the military. Osei Tutu also brought former enemies into the royal household. In one instance, after marrying the daughter of a defeated king, Osei Tutu appointed the king as chief of the royal bodyguards. In an-

other astute move, he arranged the marriage of a defeated king's niece so that her son would be the next *Asantehene*.

Osei Tutu created an elaborate system of taxation and a judicial appeal process that allowed all participating citizens to appeal to a court in Kumasi, the capital. To ensure the loyalty of the neighboring states, he established the Odwira Festival, a five-day-long gathering of Ashanti leaders in Kumasi. Historian A. Adu Boahen writes about Osei Tutu's still-heralded leadership: "He was by every standard a really great ruler, an original thinker, a statesman, a law-giver and a brilliant general, so it is not surprising that his name occupies such a place of renown in Asante [Ashanti] oral tradition."[14]

Dahomey

During the nineteenth century West Africans and Europeans alike feared the kingdom of Dahomey. As one historian puts it, "The mere mention of the name would . . . break up a crowded market in Egbado [a Yoruba settlement] and send the people seeking safety."[15] Europeans described fantastic tales of human sacrifice. They also recorded their surprise at discovering that the king used thousands of women warriors as his guards.

Dahomey began as one of several small city-states along the coast of what is now Ghana and Benin. Like all of the tribes in the region, the Fon people of Dahomey were paying tributes of slaves and gold to the Yoruba kingdom of Oyo. In the later half of the seventeenth century, the Fon rebelled, and their king, Agaja, conquered all of the surrounding states by the early stages of the eighteenth century. But the Fon were unable to defeat Oyo's army.

One of the cities to fall to Agaja was Ouidah. Agaja's conquest was important not only because the Ouidah people were bitter enemies of the Fon but also because they had been slave traders to the Europeans. A few years before the city's demise, British observer John Atkins wrote that Ouidah "is now the greatest trading place on the coast of Guinea, selling off as many slaves, I believe, as all the rest together—forty or fifty ships . . . loading their cargoes there every year."[16] Europeans turned to Agaja, expecting him to carry on the slave trade. They soon discovered that he had prohibited his own people from trading in slaves. He also began burning the European slave houses. In 1727 he imprisoned an English captain for a short time, offering to compromise by permitting the slave trade to continue, but only if the slaves were used on African soil.

Both the Oyo kingdom and European traders pressured Agaja not to upset the status quo, so he had no choice but to comply. However, the numbers of slaves being traded along "the Slave Coast"—as Europeans dubbed the region—diminished considerably. Only after the 1820s, when the Yoruba states rebelled against Oyo's authority and Great Britain stepped up its suppression of the slave trade, was Dahomey able to become totally independent from external forces and end its participation in the slave market.

Independence, however, lasted only about fifty years. The nineteenth-century competition between Great Britain and France for control over West African trade led to European intervention in the region. The French finally conquered the Dahomey kingdom in the 1890s.

Decline of the Forest Kingdoms

In the 1880s all of West Africa was under siege. European powers sought control of

Many ships like this one set sail from "the Slave Coast" of Guinea, which was the site of a flourishing slave trade with Europe in the early part of the eighteenth century.

the sources of raw materials for their economies. The main product was palm oil, the lubricant of the Industrial Revolution in Europe. It was used in soap, producing a fine lather; it was the best oil for the cotton factories in England; and it was also used as a lubricant on ships. Very few African states, though, were able to shift their own economies from slave trading to palm oil.

By then, however, the use of firearms was widespread in West Africa. As a result, Europeans and Africans frequently clashed. To guarantee that trade would continue and that European trading companies would make high profits, Europeans progressively took control over the tribal territories. By 1900 Great Britain and France ruled most of West Africa.

Chapter 4

From Colonialism to Independence

The decline of the trans-Saharan trade is directly related to the expanding European trade on the Guinea coast in the sixteenth century. Europeans came for gold and ivory. They stayed for the enormous profits from the slave trade.

When the slave trade reached its peak in the early 1800s, the African coastal states still controlled their own territory. But one of the strange ironies of history is that European rule of West Africa started only after the trade in humans gave way to the demand for palm oil, coffee, cocoa, rubber, diamonds, and other commodities.

The Slave Trade

During the fifteenth century few European traders wanted slaves. One British ship captain wrote that he was offered "certain young black women who were standing by themselves . . . which he [an African trader] told me were slaves, brought for me to buy. I made answer, We were a people who did not deal in any such commodities, neither did we buy or sell one another, or any that had our own shapes."[17]

By the eighteenth century, however, England, Holland, and France were expanding their empires into North America and Asia. England, the world's strongest sea power, sought slave labor for its colonial plantations in southern America and in the Caribbean. The slave population in Virginia alone multiplied from 4,000 in 1700 to 40,000 in the 1740s; by the time of the American Revolution, Virginia had 200,000 slaves. In 1730, about 80,000 slaves lived in North America. By 1750, the number had increased to nearly 240,000. By the American Revolution, slaves in the American colonies numbered 600,000, or about 20 percent of the entire population.

African Slavery

Slavery has existed in all parts of the world for thousands of years, even in West Africa. However, slaves in West Africa were more similar to serfs in feudal Europe than to slaves in the American

Slaves arrive in Virginia. The number of African slaves in colonial America grew dramatically in the decades before the Revolutionary War.

colonies. Slaves might work as bodyguards or stablemen for West African royal families. Many slaves fought as part of the imperial armies. Others worked as house servants. Often slaves worked their way into high status within communities.

The British governor of the colony, R. S. Rattray, wrote that among the Ashanti,

a slave might marry; own property; himself own a slave; swear an oath; be a competent witness; and ultimately become heir to his master. . . . They seemed in many cases practically the ordinary privileges of an Ashanti free man. . . . An Ashanti slave, in nine cases out of ten, possibly became an adopted member of the family, and in time his descendents so merged and intermarried with the owner's kinsmen that only a few would know their origin.[18]

Slave trading among African rulers, however, was not as beneficial as trading slaves to the Europeans. These rulers needed weapons to defend their power, and the only way they could get them was in exchange for slaves. Eventually African rulers were corrupted into escalating violence just to find slaves to trade. Thereafter, these leaders were trapped, unable to escape the pressures to discontinue the trade. This preoccupation with the slave trade and fighting caused a corresponding drop in interests in healthy economic practices. The crafts, mining, and legitimate trading declined. West Africans were no longer encouraged to develop their skills.

Some ethnic groups in the forest belt lost hundreds of thousands of people just in a couple of decades. British captain John Adams, who traded in the Niger Delta between 1786 and 1800, wrote that twenty thousand slaves a year were sold at the seaport village of Bonny. "Of these," he continued, "16,000 come from one nation, called the Ibos, so that this single nation has exported, over the past twenty years, not fewer than 320,000 of its people; while members of the same nation sold at New and Old Calabar, in the same period, probably amounted to 50,000 more."[19]

The numbers of slaves exported to the New World can only be roughly estimated. Some conservative numbers illustrate the extent of the trade: Out of an estimated 25 million exported from Africa, about 16 million survived the Middle Passage, or ship journey, across the Atlantic. In addition, as many as 10 million might have died in Africa during slave raids and the march to the sea. By 1800 half of the populations of Brazil and Venezuela were of African descent. In some parts of the southern United States, especially in South Carolina and along Virginia's coast, Africans made up the majority population.

During the nineteenth century the British led the movement to abolish the slave trade for moral and economic reasons. However, industrial expansion in Europe also played an important part in the abolition movement. When the slave trade reached its highest point, the European powers had just entered the Industrial Revolution. With new industries using machines throughout the continent, less raw labor was needed. Europeans then shifted the focus of their African trade to palm oil, cotton, and other raw products.

Slaves in Africa often had opportunities not available to those who were brought to the New World.

A Slave's Journey on Ship

At West African ports, slaves were stripped and inspected by ship captains and their officials. Once negotiations with the African sellers were complete, slaves were loaded onboard ships for the journey across the Atlantic. Many Africans tried unsuccessfully to escape while being taken in canoes to the ships.

The slaves were packed onboard so closely together that their bodies were less than an inch apart. Ship floors became so covered with waste and contamination that disease was widespread. Captains tried to keep their slaves alive for the slave market in the Americas. They brought them out on deck periodically and forced them to exercise. Women were regularly raped by the sailors. To discourage rebellion, slaves who refused to obey orders were usually tortured and thrown overboard. In one example, a ship captain killed some slaves and made the instigator of the revolt eat the heart and liver of one of the dead slaves before being thrown overboard.

As many as 15 percent died on the journey across the Atlantic. Captains carried insurance on their "cargo" to cover slave deaths during the trip. One captain, faced with a ship running short on water, threw more than one hundred slaves into the Atlantic. His investors in Europe could then claim the insurance on the lost slaves on the grounds that it was necessary for the health of the rest to get rid of some of the cargo. In the 1800s, when the trade was outlawed, the British sent patrols out to stop slave ships. This often provoked slave ship captains to throw their "cargo" overboard into the ocean rather than be stopped.

African slaves endured unspeakable conditions on their journey across the Atlantic Ocean.

Although European nations became more aggressive, at first they had no intention of establishing colonial empires. An official British government report as late as the 1860s declared that it would be too expensive and not worth the effort to govern the vast areas of Africa. Nonetheless, Europeans desired African products and were at a disadvantage when bartering in African nations that were not influenced by European monarchs. In these nations, Africans could establish the terms of trade.

Jaja of Opobo

Climate and geography also made many of the regions uninviting to European businessmen eager to set up shop in western Africa. In the Niger Delta of southern Nigeria, the swamps and mangroves seemed almost uninhabitable to Europeans. Mary Kingsley, who traveled and wrote about Africa in the late nineteenth century, described "torrential downpour of the wet-season rain, coming down night and day with its dull roar. I have known it to rain six mortal weeks in Bonny River."[20] Malaria and other tropical diseases discouraged any attempt at European settlement.

In spite of this harsh environment, West Africans had created a vibrant society there, with business skills easily adaptable to the European system of commerce. In the class structure of the Niger Delta, thousands of people were slaves, but slaves could work their way up the economic ladder and become prominent citizens.

One such man was Jaja of Opobo, one of the greatest men in Ibo history. Born a domestic slave in 1821 in the Bonny region of the Niger Delta, he proved to be a genius at the palm oil trade. Rather than stay in Bonny and fight with both the Europeans and his African competitors, Jaja relocated nearby, starting his own independent state of Opobo in 1870. Count C. N. de Cardi, who traded in the Niger Delta between 1862 and 1896, later wrote that "Opobo became, under King Ja Ja's firm rule, one of the largest exporting centres of palm oil in the Delta, and for years King Ja Ja enjoyed a not undeserved popularity amongst the white traders who visited his river."[21]

For sixteen years Jaja ruled a highly successful trading empire, outmaneuvering his rivals and the British who tried to regulate the trade. After several years of frustration, British authorities arrested Jaja and convicted him of breaking various treaty agreements. He was exiled to the West Indies, where he died in 1892.

Europeans Take Control

Jaja's story reflects several prominent features of the coming European rule. First, the Europeans rarely recognized the Africans' aptitude for business because their lifestyles were so different. They felt they had to wrest control away from Africans so that European trade would never be compromised. Europeans' primary interest was in economics—profits for their trading companies. Second,

The Niger Delta

For over two centuries, Europeans carried on extensive trade in the Niger Delta. Dozens of small, powerful "houses"—that is, large groups of families—competed for the European trade. Historian G. I. Jones includes in his book *The Trading States of the Oil Rivers*, an excerpt from Dutch trader John Barbot's report of the Bonny area of the Niger Delta in the late seventeenth century.

"[Bonny, which consists of] about three hundred houses, divided into parcels, stands in a marshy ground, made an island by some arms of the river from the main: it is well peopled with *Blacks*, who employ themselves in trade, and some at fishing . . . by means of long and large canoes, some sixty foot long and seven [foot] broad, rowed by sixteen, eighteen or twenty paddlers carrying *European* goods and fish to the upland *Blacks*; and bring down to their respective towns, in exchange a vast number of slaves, of all sexes and ages, and some large elephants teeth, to supply the *Europeans* trading in that river. Several of those *Blacks* act therein as factors, or brokers, either for their countrymen, or for the *Europeans* who are often obliged to trust them with their goods, to attend the upper markets, and purchase slaves for them."

Europeans often had to use deceptive methods to get Africans to "settle down" and accept European rules. Africans, however, often resisted European authority, sometimes with force and other times with their wits.

Despite early resistance, European military might and the advantages of trade pacified West Africa in short order. By 1900 Europeans controlled much of the African continent. They cared nothing about preserving African cultural unity. National boundaries were drawn without regard for previously established ethnic homelands. Consequently, most of the larger ethnic groups in West Africa, such as the Yoruba, Hausa, and Mande, live in several countries.

France and England ruled most of West Africa. The British used indirect rule by appointing Africans to administer British policies. As long as West Africans supplied the raw materials for British industry, the colonial governors allowed the Africans to live relatively free of interference.

The French system used assimilation, whereby West Africans could become French citizens by adopting French customs. In practice, the French employed a policy of "association," encouraging African nations to ally economically with France. Ultimately, the French governed indirectly, supporting local chiefs who backed the colonial policies.

African Independence

When African men returned to their homelands from European and American universities in the 1930s and 1940s, they campaigned for more self-government for their nations. They were joined by the hundreds of thousands of colonial soldiers returning from World War II who wanted the same freedoms they helped the Europeans defend in the war. In both French- and British-ruled West Africa, the variety of African leadership ranged from moderate negotiators to radical resisters. However, unlike other parts of Africa, West Africa experienced very little violence.

French West Africa

The French ruled most of the land area of West Africa, including the modern-day

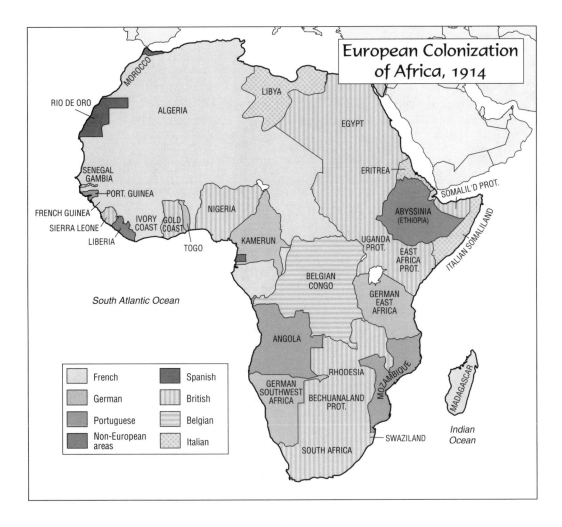

European Colonization of Africa, 1914

MOROCCO

RIO DE ORO

ALGERIA

LIBYA

EGYPT

SENEGAL
GAMBIA

ERITREA

SOMALIL'D PROT.

PORT. GUINEA

FRENCH GUINEA

NIGERIA

ABYSSINIA
(ETHIOPIA)

SIERRA LEONE

IVORY
COAST

GOLD
COAST

ITALIAN SOMALILAND

LIBERIA

TOGO

KAMERUN

UGANDA
PROT.

EAST
AFRICA
PROT.

BELGIAN
CONGO

GERMAN
EAST
AFRICA

South Atlantic Ocean

ANGOLA

RHODESIA

MOZAMBIQUE

MADAGASCAR

GERMAN
SOUTHWEST
AFRICA

BECHUANALAND
PROT.

Indian
Ocean

SWAZILAND

SOUTH AFRICA

	Legend	
French	Spanish	
German	British	
Portuguese	Belgian	
Non-European areas	Italian	

countries of Benin, Burkina Faso, Guinea, Ivory Coast, Mali, Mauritania, Niger, Senegal, and Togo. Until the mid-1950s, West African leaders under French rule hoped to establish their own large nation. These men were highly educated and were politically sophisticated.

The most respected West African leader was Leopold Senghor of Senegal, Africa's best-known poet and intellectual; another, Modibo Keita of Mali, was a Muslim scholar; Sekou Toure of Guinea claimed descent from the famous nineteenth-century West Africa warrior Samori and leaned toward Marxist solutions to political issues; and Houphouet-Boigny of Ivory Coast was a highly successful, and politically cautious, owner of a large plantation.

What emerged from this political mix was confusion, with territories guarding their individual political stature within a proposed larger union. The richer nations, such as Ivory Coast, refused to surrender self-control; the poorer nations, such as Niger, feared domination by the more prosperous ones. Add to these problems the suspicions of hundreds of diverse ethnic groups with different languages and traditions, and the union was doomed.

British West Africa

The British West African countries of Gambia, Ghana, Nigeria, and Sierra Leone followed a different path, each demanding individual nationhood that would be followed by some form of regional accord. Led by charismatic leader Kwame Nkrumah, Ghana became the first independent nation in West Africa in 1957. A radical socialist, Nkrumah returned to the Gold Coast (Ghana) after receiving his degree from Lincoln University in Pennsylvania. Nkrumah argued passionately for pan-African unity, not just independence for the Gold Coast.

Prime Minister Kwame Nkrumah waves to a crowd celebrating Ghana's independence in 1957.

But the reality of the ethnic rivalries just in West Africa alone guaranteed he would never accomplish that goal.

Freedom for the colony of Nigeria proved more complicated. Because of its huge population, many observers thought it would be impossible to balance the political power among the major ethnic groups. The Hausa/Fulani, Ibo, and Yoruba had never lived together under a single government except during British colonial rule. Eventually, three powerful men from these ethnic groups emerged as leaders of Nigeria's independence movement.

Nnamdi Azikiwe, an Ibo educated in the United States, campaigned so effectively through journalism and political activism that he is identified as "the Father of Nigerian Independence." He was joined by Obafemi Awolowo, a Yoruba, and Ahmadu Bello, a Fulani. Through tireless effort and compromise, they led Nigeria to independence in 1960.

Nnamdi Azikiwe, one of the three dynamic men who led the campaign for Nigerian independence, is welcomed to London in 1961.

The Effects of European Rule

Europeans introduced modern medicine and education to West Africa. They also created government bureaucracies that still run these nations. However, Europeans rarely appointed Africans to top administrative positions. Instead, Africans were trained as clerks and laborers. The lack of trained government officials would hinder African progress in the twentieth century.

Economically, Europeans left most West African countries without foundations to compete with other nations. They created one-crop-economies, forcing each colony to grow only one main crop for export at the expense of creating a more diverse economic foundation. Ghana, for example, was converted into a vast cocoa plantation; Senegal was pressured to grow groundnuts (peanuts), so that today 40 percent of the arable land is used for this one crop. When the world market price for these products drops, these nations are unable to recover their costs, and the standard of living declines.

European nations wanted no competition for their own manufacturing plants, so they built little industry in West Africa. The raw materials were grown or mined in Africa and were then sent to Europe for processing and refining into finished products. Europeans then sent the finished products back to West Africa for sale at inflated prices. Thus, Europeans had the best of the trade: cheap supplies of raw material and a market in which to sell the finished products. Africans were both the suppliers and the consumers.

This is the state of West African economies today. They are engaged in programs to diversify their economies. Nations such as Ivory Coast, Ghana, and Nigeria have great potential for development. Others, such as Mali and Niger, face a bleak future without bringing in some form of industry. European countries maintain ties to their former colonies, but West African nations are cautious about allowing Europeans back into African affairs.

Chapter 5

Family and Community

"Only in terms of other people does the individual [African] become conscious of his own being, his own duties, his privileges and responsibilities toward himself and toward other people."[22] These words, by professor of African religions John S. Mbiti, explain the significance of group identity to West Africans. Almost every West African feels an obligation to family, to community, and to heritage. People who have moved to the cities, for example, often return to their home villages for traditional events. And they are expected to help out financially by contributing to village projects, from building utility plants to establishing scholarships for promising young students. Even with this complex network of relationships, however, the family still provides the foundation of West African life.

Family, the Heartbeat of Society

Mbiti writes that for the African, "to die without getting married and without chil-dren is to be completely cut off from the human society, . . . to become an outcast and lose all links with mankind."[23] For West Africans, the heartbeat of society is the nuclear family: father, mother, and their children. Because polygyny—that is, having more than one wife—is common, a single household might consist of several stepmothers and half sisters and half brothers as well. They all consider them-selves part of the immediate family.

Beyond this core, however, West Africans feel a special tie to other branches of their kin: grandparents, un-cles and aunts, and cousins. This second type of kinship is called an extended family. In rural areas, where about 65 percent of the people live, these branches usually occupy separate households or compounds, and together they often make up a small village.

The Wisdom of Elders

West Africans believe that people become wiser with age. In traditional societies,

A Malian man poses with his wives. Having more than one wife is common for men in West Africa.

usually the oldest members of extended families serve on a governing council. Secret societies made up of prominent elders are also involved in regulating community affairs. No nonmember is supposed to know who belongs to these societies.

Members take oaths of silence, and in the past, they would banish or even kill anyone who violated the oath. Often, when all-male secret societies are carrying out their special ceremonies, females and children are supposed to stay indoors. In some rituals, masked members represent dead ancestors who have come back to settle serious village disputes, and the entire village will witness the events.

Women are also extended the respect due their age. As they grow older they take on more responsibilities in the family, the clan, and the village. In polygynous marriages, the senior wife is the main wife, receiving special privileges. Women often have their own organizations and advance into positions of higher authority with age.

Rearing Children

"Without children you are naked." This Yoruba proverb explains the importance of children to West Africans. Until their teenage years, children enjoy constant attention from family friends and relatives. But as they grow older, children are also expected to care for their younger brothers and sisters. In this environment, children grow up knowing they are a valued part of society.

Traditionally, boys learn farming, hunting, and fishing from their fathers. Girls spend most of their time learning domestic jobs from their mothers. Although such parental tutoring is still true in most of the region, elementary education is becoming mandatory in most West African countries. But because family survival is paramount, children are often expected to help gather food and harvest crops before attending school. The figures vary greatly according to country, but only about 30 to 40 percent of the boys and 10 to 20 percent of the girls in West Africa are able to go on to sec-

ondary school. African governments, however, see the need for more well-educated young people.

Becoming an Adult

In West Africa, boys and girls within a few years of each other undergo several tests to prepare for adult life. The most important of these is the traditional adult initiation ritual. Boys of the Mende people of Sierra Leone and Liberia, for example, join local groups of the Poro society. Its primary function is to teach boys about their roles as men in their society. The girls join a similar society called the Sande.

Among West Africans, initiation into adulthood includes challenges that stress self-control. Guinean author Camara Laye, a member of the Malinke ethnic group, later wrote about his own initiation. According to Laye, the first stage involved the "society of the uninitiated" for uncircumcised boys between twelve and fourteen years old. After gathering in the forest for song and music, they waited to meet Kondén Diara, the "lion that eats up little boys." His father told him, "you have to control your fear; you have to control yourself. Kondén Diara will not take you away. He will roar. But he won't do more than roar."[24]

On the night of Kondén Diara, Laye sat in the forest with the other uncircumcised boys of his age group. He writes, "We were on our knees with our foreheads to the ground and our hands pressed over our eyes. Kondén Diara's roaring suddenly

Naming Children

Throughout West Africa, names are given with great care. Likewise, they usually have very specific meanings. Here is a list of popular names given to Yoruba babies, as described by Diana Daird N'Diaye and Betty Belans, who work on The African Immigrant Folklife Study Project.

Name	Pronunciation	Meaning
Descriptive names		
Ajayi	Ah-jah-yee	Born face down, as if praying
Dada	Dah-dah	Born with plenty of hair
Taiwo	Tie-woe	Firstborn of twins
Kehinde	Kay-hin-day	Secondborn of twins
Idowu	Ee-dough-woo	Born after twins
Ola	Oh-la	Born after Idowu
Otunla	Oh-tune-la	Born after Ola
Etaoku	Eh-ta-oh-coo	Born after Otunla
Erioku	Air-ee-oh-coo	Born after Etaoku
Names based on the family's attachment to Yoruba deities		
Orishabiyi	Or-ee-shah-bee-yee	Deity brought this one
Ifasen	Ee-fa-sen	Ifa performs miracle
Ogunfiditimi	Oh-goon-feed-ee-teem-ee	Ogun is with me
Shangokoya	Shan-go-coy-ah	Shango does not take insults
Names reserved for royal families		
Adedayo	Ah-day-dye-yo	Crown becomes joy
Aderonke	Ah-day-wrong-kay	Object of royal adoration
Names belonging to warrior clans		
Akinkuotu	Ah-keen-coo-oh-too	Strong man or warrior does not leave the clan (boy)
Olakuotu	Oh-la-coo-oh-too	Honor or leadership pride does not leave the clan (girl)
Family names of powerful traditional doctors		
Ewegbemi	Ey-wayg-bay-me	Herbs help me
Eweji	Ey-way-gee	Herbs work

Young West Africans like these girls go through challenging initiation rituals as they enter adulthood.

burst out." Soon it was not just one lion, but "ten, twenty, perhaps thirty lions . . . uttering their terrible roars."[25] Laye, like the other boys, proved his courage by not showing the fear he felt inside.

After a short return to the village, the boys progressed to the second stage, circumcision, during which boys demonstrate their courage and ability to withstand pain. This event took one week of preparation in group dancing and singing. After the circumcision, they spent the next three weeks learning how to behave as men. Laye writes, "These lessons . . . [covered] what a man's conduct should be: we were to be absolutely straightforward, to cultivate all the virtues that go to make an honest man,

to fulfill our duties toward God, toward our parents, our superiors and our neighbors. We must tell nothing of what we learned, either to women or to the uninitiated."[26]

Marriage

West Africans believe they must get married so they can have children who will then honor their parents as elders and eventually as ancestors. Most West African societies require marriage outside of one's own clan. This strengthens ties between local groups and often serves to reduce civil strife between neighboring clans. Traditionally, a young man gets permission to marry from the woman's parents. In some societies, this involves a complicated series

Age Groups

The Ibo of eastern Nigeria provide a clear example of age-grouping. In his introductory essay in Chinua Achebe's *Things Fall Apart*, African historian Don Ohadike explains that the Ibo divide their population into age groups, which span three- to five-year intervals. Beyond this, the Ibo can be classified into three general groups: junior, middle, and senior. Junior boys under age sixteen are usually assigned "minor jobs like fetching water, cleaning footpaths, sweeping the streets and town squares, and running errands."

Ohadike writes that men between sixteen and forty are usually divided into five-year subgroups. In the past, they made up the military forces, "felled trees and cleared the bush at the beginning of each planting season. They functioned as the executive arm of the government and would apprehend fugitives."

Those over forty are members of the senior age group. They handle the judicial affairs of the village. "They usually decided when a town should go to war, how an offender should be punished, when the various agricultural cycles would open and close, and when the annual festivals would be held."

of discussions among the elders of the extended family.

Eventually the man gives gifts to the woman's parents, and maybe even to some members of her extended family. It is still common practice for the groom to pay a "bride price"—a sum of money or perhaps animals or some commodity valued by the society. In Yoruba society, if the marriage breaks up, the bride price remains with the woman's family unless the woman is judged at fault in the divorce.

A wedding day is set and a celebration planned. If the couple is Christian or Muslim, they follow the basic rites of their religion. But it is common to mix customs, so that weddings frequently include ceremonies from more than one religion. In most cases extended family members come together to share kola nuts, drink palm wine, dance, and offer advice to the newlyweds.

Community Responsibility

The web of connections and responsibilities extends far beyond the nuclear and extended family in West African societies. Over several generations the lineage becomes large and complicated. People living in the same village think of each other as kin. They are taught from early childhood that their community's welfare is linked to a set of long-practiced customs requiring them to treat each other as extended family.

Individuals pass through a series of rituals that serve to establish their identity as a member of the community. These include ceremonies related to naming and initiation into adulthood, marriage, parenthood, and social and political societies.

The key to success in life lies not in rugged individualism but in being a link in a social chain. West Africans learn at a young age that their actions must promote the welfare of the community. Sobonfu and Malidoma Some, who now live in the United States, describe the importance of community in their home country of Burkina Faso:

This Nigerian bride and groom are celebrating their wedding day accompanied by family members. West African wedding ceremonies often reflect the region's diverse religious heritage.

West African children grow up in tightly knit communities that function as extended families.

Our ancestors believed family went beyond bloodlines, and community was the core, the very substance, of human existence. . . . Everyone is family. Many different mothers nursed us as babies. Children address their age mates as sister or brother, all adults as mother or father. In fact, most . . . children don't learn who their biological parents are until they're about 5 years old. And because everyone is family, there is an immense resource of love and care. In that context, no child is ever alone.[27]

When Nigerian author Wole Soyinka was a boy, his father was the head of a Christian church, so they lived on a large compound with a spacious home. His mother constantly took in other children for weeks at a time, as if they were extended family members. Soyinka writes that

> at night, sufficient space was created on the floor [of his mother's bedroom] where a mat was spread to sleep a constantly varying assortment of children—sometimes as many as twelve—there being no more avid collector of strays. . . . We never knew her to say No to any of those parents, guardians or relations who brought their ward for "training," or simply to be cared for.[28]

Class Structure

In the traditional village, people are usually expected to follow specific social and economic roles. Those who break out of this mold could upset the delicate balance and disrupt the stability of the entire community.

The structure of the Malinke society illustrates this rigid hierarchical system. In the past, the royal family members were all-powerful. Today, although civil government has taken over the political power throughout the western Sudan, the Malinke royal families still retain their prestige and influence. Islamic scholars make up the second-highest social class. Members of this small but well-educated group often serve as government advisers and teachers.

Next comes the largest group, the farmers. Beneath them, but often attaining material wealth, come the artisans, including leatherworkers, blacksmiths, and the famous griots, or oral historian-musicians. In the past, the lowest group consisted of slaves. Today these are the servants and unskilled workers.

Other societies in West Africa tend to allow more social mobility. The Ibo in eastern Nigeria honor individual achievement more than family identity. Their traditional communities are small, independent villages, each made up of several different extended family groups. Without a central authority such as a chief or king, each village handles its own affairs through groups such as a council of elders, a council of chiefs, women's associations, secret societies, and even organizations called Age Groups based on people of similar ages.

Male and Female Roles

Among all ethnic groups, tradition requires a clear separation of roles between men and women. Sometimes the difference might relate to the stage of work performed, as in clothing. Often, spinning cotton is women's work while weaving is men's. In other cases, the two sexes might have a separate public meeting area: the stream or well for women and the town square for men.

In traditional societies, men tend and butcher animals, clear land, build houses, carve wood, smelt iron and gold, and hunt. In the urban areas, men work at all kinds of jobs, from street vendors, construction workers, and cabdrivers to store managers, teachers, and company executives. Today, as in the past, most of those responsible for governing communities are male.

Men, especially outside the large cities, are farmers. The Yoruba consider almost all farming as men's work. In most other West African societies women also farm, but custom requires men and women to grow different crops. For example, both Ibo men and women grow yams; but men grow the bigger yam called *ji*, and women grow the smaller cocoyam. Among the Malinke people, men grow millet and sorghum, and women usually grow rice.

Women's Affairs

In all West African societies the mother is the center of the home. She is responsible for an enormous variety of work, including shopping and cooking, caring for and disciplining children, and washing clothes. Women in cities and in the countryside can be seen wearing colorful head wraps and wraparound skirts and blouses and bent over two-foot-high, hollowed-out logs or barrels, pounding grain into flour for cooking. Women also are involved in crafts such as pottery and dyeing cloth.

Because Islam restricts the mixing of men and women, women in the western Sudan participate less in affairs outside the

Women in West Africa have organized effectively to promote social programs and government reforms.

home than women in the Guinea forest and coastal areas. But women in non-Muslim areas have always taken an active role in their society. In many societies, such as the Yoruba and Ibo, women traditionally run the markets, and they are not shy in expressing their opinions about economic affairs.

In Nigeria, for example, organized market women have forced governments to change laws, lower taxes, and take other measures to protect women. In 1918 the market women in Abeokuta, Nigeria, were being forced to pay higher taxes to do business. This, along with increased British control over local affairs, sparked a women's revolt. They formed the Iba Women's Union, a local group that grew into the Nigerian Women's Union in the 1920s.

In Ghana the Thirty-first December Women's Movement has about 1.5 million members. Its programs include day-care centers, tree-planting campaigns, immunization for children, family planning, and rural development. Beginning with foreign donations, the organization now receives over 95 percent of its funds from its own programs. Spokeswoman Nana Konadu Agyemang Rawlings, wife of Ghana's president, says, "We have changed the face of Ghanaian women."[29]

Today women in Muslim areas are also becoming more active. In Mali, wives from the ten-family village of Tenemakana have established a women's cooperative which pools the profits they make from selling their fruit and vegetables in markets. The members can borrow money at 9 percent interest to improve their own land with wells and fences. They have used part of the money to build schools and a clinic for their village.

Tradition and Change

Throughout West Africa traditional values are being challenged by new technologies and ideas. However, the vast majority of people still live in rural areas working the land, and they cling to customs passed on for centuries. Without losing the reinforcement of community, West Africans are beginning to adopt modern technology. The real challenge comes in adapting to the rapid pace of urbanization without losing the sense of community that has made West Africans strong in the past.

Chapter 6

Religion

The majority of West Africans practice either Islam or Christianity. But traditional religions remain a central force in people's lives. Like Christianity and Islam, traditional West African religions teach that each person has an eternal soul or spirit, and that a single creator-god is responsible for all life. Everything in the universe, from humans to a tiny grain of sand, contains a spiritual force given by the creator.

According to traditional beliefs, the universe is made up of two parts: the visible and the invisible. The visible universe consists of the material world: humans, animals, minerals, and vegetables. The invisible universe is inhabited by the spiritual beings, including the creator, lesser divinities, and a variety of spirits.

The Spirit World

Called Onyame (meaning "Fathomless Spirit") by the Ashanti and Olorun ("Owner of the Sky") and Olodumare ("the Almighty") by the Yoruba, the creator is a god beyond human understanding. While the creator watches over all things, a host of lesser divinities (*orisha* in Yoruba) were given specific responsibilities and powers by the creator over such natural forces as water, fire, and storms. There is usually a goddess in charge of the earth and a god who looks over metallurgy, or mining. Many divinities are specialized according to locality, such as a village or clan spirit who is likely a legendary ancestor.

The least-powerful members of the spirit world are the spirits of dead ancestors who have not been deified to clan or village protector. Because ancestors are closer to the creator than the living are, people try to keep in close contact with them. Calling on the wisdom of ancestors is common, and following the traditions of their ancestors helps people maintain harmony and balance between the two worlds. The goal in life, then, is to live a good life according to community customs. A person who lives a bad life will never be honored as an ancestor.

West African Divinities

Besides the supreme creator, West Africans believe in patron spirits who control various forces in the universe. People offer tribute to these divinities, but they do not worship them as the supreme god.

Storm gods. Divinities of lightning and thunder are popular in West Africa. The Songhai people tell the story of a spirit named Dongo. He was tossing an axe around in the sky when a friend made a spark. A flash of lightning struck the earth and many people in a village were killed.

Saddened, Dongo asked his mother what to do. She took him to his grandfather, who gave him a pot with water. Dongo then filled his mouth with water and sprayed it onto the dead people. They returned to life. Dongo told the people they had been punished because they had forgotten to sing his praises.

The best-known god of lightning is the Yoruba spirit Shango. All of the legends about Shango say he was a human king who toyed with a charm that brought lightning from the sky. Fire raged through many villages. In one legend many villagers were killed; in another, Shango's own family was burned to death. Shango, shamed by the killings, retreated to the forest and hanged himself.

To intimidate Shango's opponent, his supporters claimed he did not commit suicide and terrorized villagers by burning houses. The people consulted an oracle, who told them that if they offered sacrifices and publicly declared that Shango did not hang himself, the fires would cease. This they did, and the site of their sacrifice is still sacred to the Yoruba. This legend suggests that a human being, Shango, could be elevated to the level of deities.

Iron gods. In one Fon legend, Lisa is the son of Mawu, the creator. Lisa was sent to Earth with metal tools to clear the forests and teach humans how to make and use tools. Lisa is then rewarded by being named the iron god (Gu), and he is given control over the sun.

The Yoruba god of iron is Ogun. He is the powerful patron of hunters, warriors, and ironworkers. Ogun is the spirit to whom many Yoruba swear an oath in courts and when making formal contracts. They believe he administers harsh justice to those who break their word.

Earth gods. Farming is the key occupation of people all over West Africa, so it is normal that they would place great emphasis on forces that might control the earth's fertility. In Ghana, the Ashanti use the term *Asase Yaa*, "Earth Thursday," to refer to the earth spirit. On that day, no one works the land. The Ibo call the earth goddess Ani or Ala. The spirit of fertility for both the earth and women, Ani is also the source of morality for humans.

The Living Dead

The time comes, within four or five generations, when no living person will have known a particular ancestor. At this point the ancestor becomes pure spirit, no longer with a human identity. However, those still clearly remembered by the living are often referred to as the living dead. They retain personality, reputation, and even physical features. Wishing to remain "alive" in the memory of their descendants, ancestors communicate with and even appear to people on Earth to give advice and guidance.

Nigerian author Innocent Onyewuenyi compares an ancestors' "vital force" with the sun's energy: "The sun is present in its rays and heats and brightens through its rays; yet, the rays of the sun singly or together are not the sun. In the same way the 'vital force' which is the being of the ancestor can be present in one or several of the living members of his clan, through his life-giving will or vital influence, without its being diminished or truncated."[30] The vital force is a spiritual energy possessed by each individual. When people die, they get closer to the creator-god, so their spiritual energy becomes stronger and more pure. The living descendants believe that by paying respect to their ancestors, they can make use of their ancestors' spiritual force to live better lives.

Festivals and Masquerades

In West Africa almost all festivals are connected in some way to religion. The Ashanti have a calendar with nine forty-two-day cycles, called *adae*. In their villages, two days during each *adae* are designated for paying respect to the souls of the chief's ancestors. Drummers and horn blowers precede the chief's entry into a special house that shelters elaborately carved wooden stools believed to protect the souls of departed chiefs. Once the current chief offers food and drink to his ancestor, the chief returns to his courtyard

This man is preparing for a festival. West African festivals usually have links with traditional religious beliefs.

Oracles

West Africans consult oracles to learn their destinies and to appeal for help from the spirit world. Commonly, a highly trained priest or priestess is the medium for communicating with the spirits. In his famous novel *Things Fall Apart*, Chinua Achebe writes about the Agbala Oracle, also known as the Oracle of the Hills and Caves, among the Ibo:

"[People] came [to the oracle] when misfortune dogged their steps or when they had a dispute with their neighbors. They came to discover what the future held for them or to consult the spirits of their departed fathers.

The way to the shrine was a round hole at the side of a hill, just a little bigger than the round opening into a hen-house. Worshippers and those who came to seek knowledge from the god crawled on their belly . . . [into] a dark, endless space in the presence of Agbala. No one had ever beheld Agbala, except his priestess. But no one who had ever crawled into this awful shrine had come out without the fear of his power. His priestess stood by the sacred fire which she built in the heart of the cave and proclaimed the will of the god. The fire did not burn with a flame. The glowing logs only served to light up vaguely the dark figure of the priestess."

and presides over the village festival of music and dancing.

Throughout West Africa, secret societies hold frequent masquerades and festivals connected with religious functions. Usually exclusively either male or female, some initiate boys and girls into the community's traditions. Because village rules are so closely tied to traditional religious beliefs, some of these societies decide punishments and fines for people who violate village taboos. In recent years, many secret societies also have branched into economics by helping to plan and pay for roads, schools, and other village projects.

The Yoruba have dozens of these societies, but one of the best known is the Egungun (meaning "Bone" or "Skeleton") society. Its seven-day festival celebrates the return of ancestors, who then will determine if the people are living properly according to traditional values and practices. When the masqueraders go around town dancing and singing to the throbbing drums, women must go inside. If any woman sees one of the masked "ancestors," then bad luck—from blindness to death—will visit her and her family.

The all-male Awa society of the Dogon ethnic group of Mali uses a noisemaker to scare away women. A story claims that, centuries ago, a man tied a flat iron piece to a string and twirled it around, making a sound that frightened women away. This flat piece of iron or wood, called the bull-roarer, is still used today in the ritual.

Islam

Although tribal religions still have great meaning for many West Africans, the arrival of Islam had a tremendous impact on the region. Started by Muhammad in Saudi Arabia in the mid-seventh century, Islam spread rapidly throughout North Africa. By the eleventh century the Berber traders had carried Muhammad's teachings into the heart of the western Sudan. Today Islam is the religion of more than 99 percent of the people in Mauritania; over 90 percent in Senegal and Mali; over 80 percent in Gambia, Guinea, and Niger; 60 percent in Ivory Coast and Sierra Leone; 50 percent in Nigeria and Burkina Faso; 45 percent in Guinea-Bissau; 30 percent in Ghana; and 20 percent in Liberia and Togo.

Islam means "Surrender to God." Devotees read the holy book the Koran, a collection of rules and guidelines covering every aspect of living. Because Muslims believe the Koran is the transcription of

These children in Timbuktu are learning the lessons of Islam, the religion practiced by many West Africans.

The Five Pillars of Islam

The five pillars are required duties for all Muslims who are capable of carrying them out. The first pillar is the creed. Muslims begin their prayers with the words, "There is no God but Allah; Muhammad is his messenger." The second pillar declares that Muslims should pray five times a day, facing Mecca. The times of prayer are at daybreak, at noon, at midafternoon, after sunset, and in the early night. When praying together at a mosque, especially on a Friday, the Muslim holy day, an imam (prayer leader and teacher) leads the prayers. The third duty is almsgiving. All Muslims who can are expected to share their incomes with the poor, widowed, and orphaned. The fourth pillar is fasting. During the month of Ramadan, the ninth month in the lunar calendar, Muslims fast during daylight to commemorate the month that Muhammad received his first visit from the archangel Gabriel. At the end of the month they celebrate with a great feast. The final pillar is the pilgrimage, or *hajj*. Those who can afford it are required to make a journey to Mecca to perform religious rituals. The journey must take place during the twelfth month of the lunar year.

God's messages to Muhammad, all Muslims follow some of the five pillars given in the scripture. These include the creed that there is only one god, the observance of daily prayer, a duty to help the poor, fasting during the Muslim holy month, and the making of a pilgrimage to the Muslim holy city of Mecca.

African Adaptation

The largest ethnic groups practicing Islam are the Hausa and the Fulani. Although they have retained a few of their African traditions, they mostly follow Islamic customs. Some ethnic groups in West Africa mix more of their own traditional beliefs with Islam. The Nupe in northern Nigeria adhere to only some of the five pillars,

such as daily prayers and fasting. Even though they usually say their Muslim prayers in Arabic, they say their personal prayers in their native language.

Wolof men in Senegal pray for rain at the Muslim mosque, but if rain fails to come, the women will resort to tradition and "perform a rain dance, dressed up in rags, or in men's clothes, wearing ornaments made from rubbish. They then go out of the village in procession, and the children gather branches of trees or shrubs, and on their return beat the grave of the founder of the village with their branches."[31]

The Yoff, a small ethnic group living near Dakar, Senegal, are usually strict Muslims, but they are famous throughout the region for their traditional healing ritual called *ndeup*. The Yoff believe that mental illnesses are caused when an evil spirit enters a person. The Yoff priest exorcises the evil spirit by sacrificing a chicken or cow and calling on a guardian spirit to enter the victim. The person being treated usually goes into a trance, and the evil spirit is drawn out by the priest. People not just from Senegal but also from Gambia, Mali, and Guinea-Bissau come for this healing.

Because Islam and traditional African religions share many beliefs, Muslim West Africans have no problem mixing the religions. For example, Islam allows a man to have four wives, and the practice of polygyny is common throughout the region. West Africans believe that many different

During the nineteenth century the influx of Christian missionaries had a major impact on West African life.

spirits exist and that they can sometimes appear to and influence humans. Likewise, Islam has long taught that spirits such as angels, genies, and devils exist and impact human life.

Christianity

The other religion that has changed West African life is Christianity. As early as the sixteenth century, the kingdom of Benin had converts to Christianity. Portugal's representative to the kingdom of Benin wrote in 1516 that the *oba* of Benin "gave his son and some of his noblemen—the greatest in his kingdom—so that they might become Christians; and also he ordered a church to be built in Benjm [Benin City]; and they made them Christians straightway; and also they are teaching them to read, and your highness will be pleased to know that they are very good learners."[32]

Missionary activity only became a major force, however, during the nineteenth century. European missionary groups, such as the Roman Catholic White Fathers and the Church Missionary Society (Anglican Church) of Great Britain, went to West Africa as an extension of the anti-slavery movement. Besides preaching the gospel, they studied West African languages, introduced up-to-date medical treatment, and offered modern education.

However, Christian missionaries also taught West Africans that their traditions were sinful. Africa was called "the Dark Continent" because the Europeans were unable to understand Africans' religious ideas. Missionaries condemned such important customs as initiation ceremonies, "pagan" dancing, the bride price, polygyny, secret societies, and ancestor worship.

Among those spreading the Christian message were former American slaves. Perhaps the best known was Bishop Samuel Adjai Crowther, a Yoruba who translated and transcribed parts of the Bible, compiled a Yoruba-English dictionary, and wrote a Yoruba grammar book in the mid–nineteenth century. He had been kidnapped in 1822 when he was a teenager and sold to a white slaver. A British warship intercepted the slave ship on the high seas and brought the captured Africans, including Crowther, to Freetown, Sierra Leone. Educated in a mission school, he earned a college degree and became a clergyman in 1843. In 1845 he returned to Yorubaland and founded the Niger Mission in 1857. He became the first modern black bishop in 1864.

West African Christianity

As with Islamic practices, West Africans have little problem mixing long-established customs with Christian teachings. Traditional medicine and exorcism are defended as healing through God's power, and the belief in the power of the Holy Spirit coincides with spirit possession in traditional West African society. Some groups tie their own history to Christian tradition. In Nigeria, the Church of Orunmila claims that the deity Orunmila was actually God's prophet sent to the Yoruba people.

Whereas many Europeans tend to separate religion from other areas of life, West Africans seek a church that reinforces their own traditional values of community. The result is an enormous variety of independent sects breaking away from central Christian churches to form local groups of worshipers. By shifting the focus of power away from European leadership, West African Christians become more credible in social and political affairs.

Religion Today

In West Africa it is impossible to separate one's culture from his or her traditional religious beliefs. Wande Abimbola, who has studied the contemporary religious practices of the Yoruba, writes, "To a striking degree, traditional practices have been retained by those who have embraced Christianity and Islam, and they still play an important role in the community generally."[33]

Yushau Sodiq, professor of Islamic studies at Texas Christian University, explains that

the Yoruba religion . . . is a mixture of many things. However, the Yoruba are . . . utilitarian in their beliefs. They seek help from "anywhere" when they are in need. If Islam supplies their need, they apply Islam, if Christianity

Rescued from a slave ship by the British, Samuel Adjai Crowther went on to become the first modern black bishop in 1864.

provides their quest, they go for it. . . . The people in West Africa [are] . . . driven by needs in their beliefs. . . . Religion is for this life and thus the life must be enjoyed to its fullest.[34]

The ritual steps in life, such as naming ceremonies, initiation rites, marriage, ancestral shrines, and funeral rituals, are as popular today as ever. In addition, West

Africans still look to diviners and traditional medicine to solve personal problems and diseases. Diviners say they can predict future events by their special ability to communicate with supernatural powers. But the number who practice traditional religions exclusively has declined dramatically.

In recent decades, however, a revival of traditional religious practices has spread throughout West Africa. Nigeria, especially, has promoted this renewal with national festivals, formal courses on traditional religions in universities, and a national policy encouraging traditional beliefs.

Chapter 7

The Arts

From their earliest years, children in West Africa are surrounded by singing, dancing, and drumming. As African scholar Elimo P. Njau writes, "African art and music were so much part and parcel of the daily life of the community that when you talked about art and music you actually talked about the people themselves, their daily activities, their day-to-day aspirations as a community, their joys together, the enemies they fought together and the tears they shed together."[35]

In art, West Africans tend to prefer some form of abstraction—usually exaggeration—to depict the spirit or life force residing in most traditional art objects. They also look for balance or symmetry between the parts. But whatever style is followed, most West Africans judge art by its usefulness: It is created to serve a specific purpose, usually to evoke a spirit.

Music combines with art and literature to form a unified trio in West African creative expression. All performers present stories and expect active participation from their audiences. The tension and potential challenge leads to creative interaction between the performer and the audience.

Sculpture

Traditional sculpture can range from small animal figures to life-size representations of humans, from elaborately carved doors to Ashanti royal stools. Although most sculpture is carved from hardwoods such as ebony, mahogany, and teak, West Africans have excelled in bronze, ivory, and stone as well. The city of Benin in Nigeria is renowned for its bronze sculpture. The Edo people were casting bronze by the lost-wax process over a thousand years ago. Remarkably realistic statues, masks, and plaques added a special richness to the palaces of their kings and aristocrats.

Figures, colors, forms, levels of abstraction—just about every quality in a sculpture is regulated by both the patron and the community standards for art. Many figures are carved to pay tribute to ancestors. Walking staffs and commemorative statues are popular with those holding prestigious offices.

Fertility dolls are popular with many West African women. Often, pregnant Ashanti women carry the foot-high *akua mma* fertility doll. African art historian

Frank Willett writes that the *akua mma* doll portrays "the Ashanti ideal of beauty: a long neck and round flat face with a high forehead and a small mouth." The Ashanti believe that "expectant mothers . . . should not look upon any deformity (even a badly carved figure) for fear their child should

Music is an integral part of life in West African communities.

resemble it. Conversely, by gazing up [at] these expressions of idealized beauty [the *akua mma*] the child is encouraged to be beautiful too."[36]

Masks

The West African people are famous for their great variety of masks. Some are worn over the face, some on top of the head so the mask's face points toward the sky, and others on top of the head like headdresses. Masks range in size from the heavy *nimba*, which is worn on the shoulders of the Baga people in Guinea, to masks that barely cover a person's face.

Most West African societies believe animals possess a life force, so using animal masks enables people to take on the spiritual strength of a particular animal. Sometimes, the masks combine human and animal characteristics, suggesting people's ability to control the power of animals.

For the most part, masks hold the cosmic energy of supernatural forces. But masks take on meaning only as a part of the entire ceremony, with the dance and accompanying music. In societies that depend on nature's cycle for a comfortable life, any unnatural event is an offense to the creator and spiritual forces. To appease the spirits and restore harmony between

Animal masks like this one representing a hyena are thought to endow their wearers with the animals' spiritual power.

the earth and the spiritual world, West Africans often hold masquerades that include masked dancers.

Dancing and Festivals

Most dancing falls into one of four varieties, according to its main purpose. The most common dance is related to religious rituals. These include worship of deities and seasonal events such as planting and harvesting. A second type of dance is ceremonial, marking the installation, coronation, or funeral of a chief or dignitary. A third type is related to the life cycles of people, from birth and naming to marriage and funerals. Finally, dance performances are held to entertain, including some masquerades and acrobatics.

Mali's famous Dogon dancers perform wearing traditional masks.

This musician from Guinea holds a kora, an instrument whose twenty-one strings produce a sound similar to that of a harp.

ing place in family shrines. Because the culture is changing so rapidly, most members of the younger generation know little about this dance. Today there is one version for the traditional ritual and another for entertaining tourists.

The Dama dancers wear masks drawn from a wide range of subjects. Some represent popular animals such as birds, rabbits, bulls, and antelopes; others reflect a variety of occupations, including merchants, hunters, and teachers. Each mask is associated with a specific choreographed dance, from which the dancers will improvise. The most famous mask is the *sirige* (or "house") mask, which is worn on the dancer's head and stands twenty feet high. The dancer performs spinning and jumping movements, bending forward and backward until the tip of the *sirige* touches the ground.

Many dances that originated centuries ago as important religious rituals are performed more for entertainment today. Mali's Dogon males are world-famous for their Dama ceremonial dances. Conducted by a secret society every two or three years, the dance guides souls to their rest-

Traditional Music

African music scholars Ayo Bankole, Judith Bush, and Sadek H. Samaan write that without music, "the people cannot properly create poetry, record history, educate children, celebrate at festivals, praise or abuse, entertain, marry or even die."[37] By the age of five, children in Yoruba society have learned basic dance steps for festivals, and they move on to choral responses to folktales and songs. They would never be accepted into their community without this knowledge.

The typical musical instruments, found in endless variations throughout West Africa, are the xylophone, *kora*, *ngoni*, and drum. The xylophone, or *balaphone*, is made up of long wooden keys about twenty inches long, which are joined by threads; small hollowed out calabashes (gourds) are attached to the bottom of the keys to amplify the sound. The kora, on the other hand, is a stringed instrument, somewhat like a large banjo. To produce its harplike sound, the musician holds the rounded gourd, which is about two feet in diameter, in his lap and strums on two rows of twenty-one strings (eleven on one row and ten on the other) with his thumb and forefinger. The wooden neck, which is about three feet long, points away from the player. The *ngoni* is another banjolike instrument with three to five strings. It is boat-shaped and is carved from a tree trunk.

Drums

Drums can be heard daily throughout West Africa, from the isolated village marketplace in the Sahel to the steaming urban centers along the coastline. They are the major instruments in traditional African festivities. Although almost everyone raised in West Africa learns to drum, only a few specially trained drummers actually perform for the public.

Drummers fall into two main categories: master drummers and common entertainers. The professional drummer usually comes from a family with a long line of drum masters. One such Yoruba family is the House of Ayan. A young trainee learns the intricate rhythms, melodies, harmonies, and intonations of all of the percussion instruments. Just as crucial to success, he will also learn the history of his people. Bankole, Bush, and Samaan explain that the most respected

Drum Making

Drums are made by professional craftsmen. Before cutting the tree, the drum maker must pacify the spirit of the tree being used. Authors Jen Kriesel, Brent Janaky, and Brian Herro describe the process in their essay "The Drum Language."

"[The Ashanti drum maker] throws an egg on the trunk and speak[s] the following words, 'I am coming to cut you down and carve you, receive this egg and eat, let me be able to cut you and carve you, do not let the iron cut me, do not let me suffer in health.' [He then pours rum on the tree just before he cuts it.] Next, a fowl is killed and placed on the tree stump and the tree is hollowed. The tree is dragged out of the forest and eggs and rum are again offered to the spirit."

drummer knows "how to communicate more to his listener. . . . His aim is to touch their hearts and move them, and it is this quality in his art that is judged to be the most important."[38]

Master drummers both perform and teach with their musical skills. Because of their intimate knowledge of the people's history and customs, master drummers perform at the more important festivals. Their role is more important than just playing music to entertain. They also help to preserve and teach their people's traditions through music.

The more common drummers throughout West Africa are members of drumming groups trained to entertain. They train for about five years before being considered masters of their trade. These groups entertain for every conceivable occasion. Among the Mandinka in southern Senegal and Gambia, for example, they perform at naming ceremonies for children and initiation ceremonies for boys and girls. They also provide music for weddings, clubs and secret societies, wrestling matches, evening dances, and even rice transplanting and farmwork.

These drummers in the Ivory Coast have spent years learning the skills they need to perform at ceremonies and community events.

Griot Music and the Blues

In his "Griots of West Africa, an Introduction Essay," music critic Robert Palmer describes the close relationship between American blues and the music played and sung by the griots.

"Blues scholar Samuel Charters in particular has constructed a genealogy for the blues in which Griot music figures prominently. 'The African musicians who correspond most closely to blues singers are the griots of the tribes of northwest Africa. . . .'

[The guitar, banjo, and fiddle] have long been traditional among West African Griots. The melodies sung by Griots, though they often have been influenced by the Islamic call to prayer, often resemble blues melodies—modal or scale structures are pentatonic, with areas of pitch-play, especially flattening, around specific intervals—the third, sometimes the fifth or seventh. These variously flattened notes correspond to the so-called 'blues notes' and the pentatonic scale corresponds to one frequently encountered in blues."

The Talking Drum

Most major West African languages are tonal—that is, the meaning of words vary according to the intensity of the tone. The talking drum is designed to mimic the variety of tones of the spoken word. Combining tones, rhythm, and pacing, drummers are able to send messages, repeat familiar stories, and present variations on themes. In fact, for the Yoruba Ayan drummers, anything that can be spoken can be drummed by supplementing the Yoruba talking drum, called *iya-ilu* (or "mother drum"), with different kinds of drums.

Griots

Telling stories through music is an ancient tradition throughout West Africa. One of the most famous types of performers is the griot. As a minstrel, a praise singer, oral historian, and professional musician, the griot traditionally served the kings of ancient Mali. However, because griots were considered tradesmen, serving others, their class status was low.

The job is difficult, however. Besides being a highly skilled musician and singer, a successful griot must know the long history of a community and keep up with current events. As a result, most are born into griot families and are taught the trade from a young age. Although women can be griots, they usually become one by marrying into a griot's family. In these cases, women are often the main singers while the men play the instruments.

Modern griots play many different instruments, but they still concentrate on the three traditional instruments: *kora*, *ngoni*, and *balaphone*. Many have gone on to fame as entertainers. Until his death in 1987, Banzumana Sissoko was one of Mali's "most revered and beloved . . . griot[s] of the century. . . . [He] could virtually bring affairs in Mali to a halt when he went on the national radio to sing and play his large, deep-toned ngoni,"[39] according to *kora* player David Gilden, leader of his own African music trio. Others have formed groups to record their music. One of the best-known today is a Malian group formed by Basekou Kouyate (who plays the *ngoni*), Toumani Diabate (*kora*), and Keletigui Diabate (*balaphone*).

Popular Music

West Africans are active participants on the world stage in all forms of popular music, from highlife and Sahel pop to Afro-beat (Afro-pop) and juju; from hip hop and gospel to reggae and jazz. Vocalists often sing in many languages, and musicians perform on several different instruments. Frequently, their singles and albums become international hits. The most successful artists tour Europe, Asia, and the Americas and record with musicians and singers from outside Africa.

The best-known music found throughout West Africa is highlife. This mix of European foxtrot, Caribbean sound, and African rhythms began in the 1920s in urban Ghana. But it spread quickly throughout the region. The "King of Highlife," saxophonist and trumpeter Emmanuel Tettey Mensah, says of the music: "We evolved a music type thereafter relying on basic African rhythms. . . . No one really can lay claim to its creation. It had always been there entrenched in West African culture. What I did was give highlife world acceptance."[40]

A blend of Cuban and authentic African sounds, Sahel pop is especially strong in Mali, Senegal, Gambia, and Guinea. One of the best-known musicians and singers is Youssou n'Dour of Senegal, who combined Afro-Cuban rhythms, Wolof talking drums, and American blues and rock music to create what is called the *mbalax* style of Sahel pop music. Singer Oumou Sangare, a young woman from Mali, has made Wassoulou music famous. Noted for its blues rhythms and Arab melody, this style of Sahel pop is named after her home region of southern Mali.

Mali's Salif Keita, nicknamed "the Golden Voice of Africa," is popular throughout the world. U.S. musician Carlos Santana has said of Keita's famous album *Soro*, "This should be number one in every country [in all styles and genres of music]."[41] Keita's music combines traditional griot music, African drums, Cuban and Latin rhythms, and Islamic sounds.

The controversial musician Anikulapo Kuti, popularly known as Fela, created the Afro-beat style in the late 1960s. He fused jazz saxophone styles, long instrumental improvisation, and funky African beats. His fame partly derives from his strong protest against government and police corruption. One of the best-known Afro-beat musicians in Nigeria today is Sonny Okosun, who interjects a strong reggae beat to his music.

Sahel pop music star Youssou n'Dour combines African sounds with musical elements rooted in Cuba and America.

Another popular music style throughout West Africa is juju, which combines refined guitar, strong vocal harmonies, and traditional drums. In the 1920s the Yoruba incorporated their traditional talking drums with the palm-wine guitar style (Hawaiian sound). In the 1950s and 1960s, Nigerian I. K. Dairo formed his own orchestra using Western instruments, including steel guitars and accordions. Today Nigerians Sunny Ade and Ebenezer Obey are two of the more popular juju musicians.

Literature

The tradition of the griot is just one branch of the ancient art of storytelling in West Africa. Children still learn about their culture by listening to adults tell stories. In rural areas, small groups of people gather around fires in the evening and entertain each other with stories. But the audience does not sit around passively; they jump in and respond to the storyteller with praise and laughter, challenging and correcting. No story is repeated exactly the same as before

Popular West African Music Stars

Senegal's Youssou n'Dour was named "African Artist of the Century" by *Folk Roots* magazine. He began performing on stage at the age of twelve, and by his mid-teens he was a regular singer with Senegal's famous Star Band. In 1981 he formed his own group, now called the Super Etoile. Singing in English, French, Fulani, Serer, and Wolof, his voice covers almost five octaves.

His success is phenomenal, having teamed up with musicians such as Paul Simon, Peter Gabriel, and Branford Marsalis. In the late eighties, n'Dour starred alongside Gabriel, Bruce Springsteen, Sting, and Tracy Chapman on the Amnesty International Human Rights Tour. In 1992 he produced in his own Dakar Xippi Studio the album *Eyes Open*, which was nominated for a Grammy Award.

Another major Senegalese star is Oumou Sangare. Her song lyrics cover the concerns of African women, from freedom of choice in marriage to remaining childless. According to journalist Maria McCloy, in the *Electronic Mail & Guardian*, Sangare told *Beat* magazine, "*Je chante pour les femmes* [I sing for the women]. I'm not against men, I adore them all. But we want to defend the rights of women."

In 1986, at age eighteen, she toured the Caribbean and Europe with a twenty-seven-piece folklore troupe. In 1989 her first recording, *Moussoulou (Women)*, sold more than two hundred thousand copies.

This album started the Wassoulou music rage in Senegal.

In addition to Wassoulou music, reggae has long been popular in West Africa. Billed as the successor to reggae star Bob Marley, Alpha Blondy from Ivory Coast blends reggae with traditional African sounds to come up with his own unique music. His grandmother nicknamed him Blondy, meaning "Bandit," when he was a boy in the 1950s. He studied English in New York City at Columbia University, but he spent most of his evenings in reggae clubs in Harlem. Upon returning to Abidjan, he began singing about police brutality and other social issues, and he became an immediate success.

During the 1980s his albums were top sellers not only in Ivory Coast but also throughout the world. His 1985 release *Apartheid Is Nazism* has been called "a hymn to peace and freedom"; however, in a 1993 interview with Mitsuro Hamamoto of *Drum* magazine, Blondy further defined his music.

"My songs are all really love songs. When I talk about God, I talk about godly love. When I talk about politicians having come together to make changes for the future generation, it's also a way for preaching love. All we do here on earth or somewhere else, it's around love and being loved. That's what I think the world needs, and we have to give that chance to our children's children—for the future generations, you see."

because the teller is constantly interacting with the audience.

Folktales and Proverbs

The best-known stories are folktales, often ones with animals as main characters. Generally, these tales illustrate proper and improper behavior by indirect criticism. Other stories are dilemma tales, with open-ended conclusions that initiate discussion. These methods enable people to consider their own behavior without being embarrassed in front of the community.

Animals, such as the spider among the Ashanti and the hare among the Tiv in Nigeria, are used to highlight how even clever people fail because of character flaws. As explained by African folklore scholar Roger D. Abrahams, these animals are versions of the trickster, whose "personal habits always betray him, as they betray all of us for what we are."[42] The trickster represents human nature at its best—ambitious for knowledge, and at its worst—a greediness that brings on defeat.

One of the more common trickster characters throughout West Africa is the tortoise. The Yoruba call him Ijapa. The gods have put all the world's wisdom into one large calabash. One day Ijapa decides he wants to be the smartest creature on earth, so he steals the calabash. He rushes back to Earth and as he hurries along the road to his home he runs into a huge tree fallen on the road. Ijapa panics and bumps against the trunk over and over again, but the calabash is so big, it prevents him from climbing over the tree. He becomes so angry that he slams the calabash on the ground. The calabash breaks open and all the wisdom contained inside flies out. And ever since wisdom has been spread throughout the world.

West Africans also relay values about life through proverbs. Among the Yoruba, proverbs are usually offered by elders. If a younger person wants to recite a proverb in the presence of an elder, the younger person must ask permission.

The Agni people of southeastern Ivory Coast have many interesting proverbs that teach the values of their society. One says, "The chicken perspires, but you can't see it because of the feathers." This suggests that rich people (covered by feathers in the proverb) experience trouble in this world just like the poor. The Ashanti say, "You do not need a big stick to break a cock's head." This proverb is similar to the Western saying, "Don't make a mountain out of a molehill."

Popular Writing

Hundreds of West African writers, poets, and playwrights have received international acclaim. The first main group emerged during the 1940s with degrees from universities in Great Britain, France, and the United States. Writing in English or French, they usually were criticizing European colonial rule.

Ibo author Chinua Achebe is commonly referred to as "the Inventor of African Literature." Achebe's *Things Fall Apart*, a novel about his people's first contact with Christian missionaries, has sold over 8 million copies in fifty different languages.

Senegal's first president, Leopold Senghor (pictured, center), with cast members at the Senegalese National Theater, is a celebrated poet.

Nigeria is also home to the Yoruba dramatist, poet, and author Wole Soyinka, who won the 1986 Nobel Prize for literature. Additionally, the first president of Senegal, Leopold Senghor, became West Africa's best-known poet.

Many renowned female writers have emerged since the 1960s. In Nigeria, Flora Nwapa gained world attention with her novel *Efuru*, a story about a strong, independent woman in a male-dominated society. Another female author, Buchi Emecheta, writes of the conflict between a modern woman and the traditional community in *The Joys of Motherhood*. Recently, the Women Writers Association in Nigeria published an anthology of new women's writing titled *Breaking the Silence*.

Film

Senegal's Ousmane Sembene directed the first commercial film in postindependent (1960s) Africa. By 1969 West Africa held its first international film festival. The

Pan-African Film and Television Festival, located in Ouagadougou, Burkina Faso, attracts filmmakers from throughout Africa and the African diaspora (the descendants of Africans throughout the world). Several West African filmmakers have won awards at the prestigious Cannes Film Festival in France. They include Burkina Faso's Souleymane Cissé, Idrissa Ouedraogo, and Gaston Kaboré.

Renaissance

Beginning with anticolonialist views prior to the mid-sixties, West African artists, musicians, and writers have graduated to more African issues, such as conserving the environment. Nigerian Bruce Onobrakpeya, for example, has created a series of prints called Sahelian Masquerade, which he calls a prayer to the gods to make people change their living habits so the Sahel region will prosper again.

With their own traditional aesthetics, West Africans are blending influences from Asia, Europe, and the Americas. As a result, they are offering a new blend of artistic expression to which people around the world can relate.

Chapter 8

The Future of West Africa

The majority of West Africans still live in tiny rural villages. Like their parents and grandparents, they manage with little income—perhaps thirty to fifty dollars a month. Most live rent-free in small mud-walled or sun-baked clay huts that they have built. They grow much of their own food, draw water from a village well or a nearby river or lake, and cook over a wood fire. And their lives are enriched with a deep respect for family and community, interacting with dozens of close relatives and friends.

Unfortunately, this portrait is tainted by unsanitary conditions for the majority, a sad reality in both rural and urban areas. In a human development report issued in 1999 by the United Nations, eleven of the thirty "least livable" countries in the world are in West Africa. They include Sierra Leone (ranked #1), Niger (#2), Burkina Faso (#4), Guinea-Bissau (#7), Mali (#9), Gambia (#12), Guinea (#14), Benin (#20), Ivory Coast (#21), Senegal (#22), and Nigeria (#29).

Unhealthy Conditions

Annually, tens of millions of West Africans suffer from diseases such as tuberculosis, malaria, African river blindness (onchocerciasis), diarrhea and dysentery, and HIV/AIDS. According to the United Nations Children's Fund, (formerly UNICEF), most West Africans born in 2000 have a life expectancy of only forty-five to fifty years.

For ten of the nations in West Africa, infant mortality rates ranged between 10 percent and 20 percent in 1998. Although high, these numbers show encouraging progress since 1960. All countries have reduced their infant deaths, and some by more than half. Gambia's rate has dropped from 20.7 percent in 1960 to 6.4 percent in 1998. Other impressive reductions have occurred in Mali, from 29.3 percent to 14.4 percent; Ivory Coast, from 19.5 percent to 9 percent; and Senegal, from 17.3 percent to 7 percent. Other countries with infant mortality rates under 10 percent include Cape Verde, Ghana, and Togo.

Perhaps the most dispiriting of all figures is the mortality rate for children under age five. Of the thirty world nations with the highest child mortality rates, twelve are in West Africa; and Sierra Leone's 30 percent is at the top of the list. Niger ranks third with 28 percent; followed by Mali, fifth, with 24 percent; Liberia, sixth, with 23.5 percent; Guinea-Bissau, eleventh, with 20.5 percent; Guinea, fourteenth, with 19.7 percent; and Nigeria, fifteenth, with 18.7 percent.

This hut made of mud and thatch is typical of the housing used by most rural West African families.

But there is a hopeful trend in this category as well. Since 1960 most West African nations have reduced their child mortality rates by more than half. In 1960, 30 percent or more of the children in almost every West African nation died by their fifth year. By 1998 all but five nations had cut their child mortality rates below 20 percent. Two of the more dramatic improvements occurred in Gambia and Mali, which lowered their rates from 36.4 percent to 8.2 percent and 51.7 percent to 28 percent, respectively.

One of the reasons for high mortality rates among children is malnutrition. Vitamin and mineral deficiencies, especially A, D, iodine, and iron, are common in both rural and urban areas. Among mothers, malnutrition leads to babies with low birth weights, brain damage, physical and intellectual retardation, and other serious problems that immediately handicap newborns. The percentage of children under five who are undernourished is about 44 percent in Mali, 35 percent in Niger, 30 percent in Ghana, 25 percent in Ivory Coast, and 21 percent in Senegal.

A person need only walk through most rural parts of West Africa and many urban areas to discover another major cause of poor health among the people: unsanitary living conditions. The United Nations estimates that the percentage of people in the area who have access to adequate sanitation ranges from a low of 6 percent in Mali to a high of 65 percent in Senegal. Most of the countries range between 25 and 40 percent. Access to safe water is a related obstacle to good health. In war-torn Sierra Leone, only about 34 percent of the people can find suitable drinking water. Senegal ranks the highest in the region, with 81 percent of its people getting safe water. The range for the rest of West Africa is between 40 and 60 percent.

The figures illustrate the severity of these problems. They also suggest that the transition out of a slow-paced, preindustrial farming and herding society is complicated. Along with advanced technology comes the displacement of large groups of people, the breakdown of extended families, and clashes between different ethnic groups.

Urban Migration

To support their families in the rural areas of West Africa, millions of people become migrant workers. Some people travel hundreds of miles from their homes to work on cocoa or rubber plantations; others take unskilled work at construction sites in the cities. Millions end up trying to sell cheap consumer goods on street corners. Migrants tend to stay in urban areas rather than return home. Thus, the number of urban residents in West Africa has doubled in the last fifty years, reaching 40 percent by the beginning of the twenty-first century. Already overcrowded, cities have no facilities for them, so living conditions are unhealthy, often with little or no electricity or plumbing. Huge areas of cities become congested, polluted, and crime-ridden.

Even West Africans with steady jobs and middle-class status are hard-pressed to make ends meet. Many have to live as Clement Ouattara lives, with fifteen people in a small rented apartment. A gas station manager in Abidjan, the largest city in Ivory Coast, Ouattara barely provides for his extended family: his wife, their five children, and eight nephews and cousins.

Washington Post journalist Stephen Buckley, who interviewed Ouattara, writes, "The eight nephews and cousins in the house came for a variety of reasons, and nearly all have been there several years. Two came because they needed a place to stay during their university years; others

This young Nigerian girl is healthy, but many West African children suffer from malnutrition.

needed shelter while they sought work; a teenage nephew sought refuge from a man in his village who threatened to kill him."[43] With his monthly income of five hundred to six hundred dollars, they eat regularly and have money to send their children to school. However, Ouattara is unable to save for the family's future.

The highest unemployment rates are among West Africans who have only completed an elementary education. These young people flocked to cities expecting to find jobs. However, without technical or vocational training, they are not qualified for fields requiring specialized skills, such as health care, mechanics, engineering, advanced agriculture, and accounting.

Education and Literacy

Of the four criteria used for the UN ranking of least livable nations, two are adult literacy and school enrollment. Six of the ten countries in the world with the lowest adult literacy rates are in West Africa; Burkina Faso has the lowest rate at 18 percent. Several of the countries have lower than 40 percent adult literacy. People who cannot read or write are likely to continue living in unsanitary conditions, clinging to their old ways of life without hope for improvement.

Progress will come only from educating the young. However, millions of children come from poor, illiterate families who keep their children at home to work. As a result, school attendance is low in many of these countries. In Niger only one out of every three school-age children attends elementary school; of these students, the average time spent in school is only a couple of years. The same problem exists in Liberia, Mali, Sierra Leone, and Burkina Faso, where fewer than half of all eligible children attend elementary school.

In Ghana, by contrast, over 77 percent attend elementary school, and Ghana's adult literacy rate is around 65 percent. Although not the richest nation in Africa, Ghana has taken huge steps toward economic and political stability. In Nigeria almost 90 percent of school-age children attend at the elementary level, and the country has an adult literacy rate of nearly 60 percent.

Other countries are also making progress in elementary-education attendance. Senegal and Ivory Coast are near 70 percent attendance today. Even the poorer nations are making strides in this area. In Mali, for example, the Woman's Cooperative has become a leader in education, building and staffing hundreds of local schools during the 1990s. According to Timm Harris, from the U.S. Agency for International Development, "[In 1998] 46.5% of Mali's children attend primary school, and the literacy rate, 19% seven years ago, is now 32%."[44]

West African governments understand the importance of expanding education. With a higher percentage of educated citizens participating in their economic and political life, their countries can make huge strides toward solving domestic problems.

Improved education for children like these girls in a Senegal elementary school will mean a brighter future for their countries.

Deforestation and Desertification

For people stuck in their subsistence farming and animal-grazing lifestyles, the future looks bleak. West African grazing and farm lands are shrinking rapidly. And human abuse of the land is a major cause.

When people clear forests so the land can be used for agriculture, they change the entire ecosystem. More direct sunlight heats the ground faster and dries out the land. Because much of the vegetation has been eliminated, there is less water to evaporate. The long-term effects are severe: soil deterioration and erosion. In ad-

dition, animals and plants that have thrived in the thick forests disappear.

Even more critical is the problem farther north in the Sahel and along the fringes of the Sahara Desert. For decades, ecologists have written about the dire consequences of the southward expansion of the desert, a process called desertification. Climate changes such as long droughts are contributing causes. But most of the deterioration comes from the way people use the land.

Throughout the region, people raise cattle. Some people are nomadic, such as the Borroroje, or "Cow," Fulani in Nigeria, who annually move their herds hundreds of miles north and south as the seasons change. Overgrazing robs what little vegetation exists in the Sahel.

Overcultivation also destroys the soil. Growing the same crops on the same plot of land year after year depletes the soil of nutrients. Add in the arid desert climate, with hot winds that blow away the topsoil, and farmers are unable to grow enough to provide for their families. The men often migrate to cities looking for work, usually leaving their families behind.

Unifying Ethnic Groups

Men and women, skilled and unskilled, are flooding the already crowded West African cities. There, they discover that good jobs are scarce. As a result, masses of unemployed and underemployed men and women from dozens of separate cultures compete for low-paying jobs in sweltering tropical climates.

In the cities, people tend to cluster in neighborhoods populated by others from either their own ethnic group or region. Traditional distrust between these groups intensifies in the teeming urban areas. Often the power to distribute government money for public works and jobs is controlled by a single ethnic group. The people in power, then, frequently help out their own ethnic or regional groups, without regard to merit. Consequently, those left out sometimes resort to rioting to protest their condition. They lash out at anyone belonging to rival ethnic groups or regions.

Nigeria, with over 120 million inhabitants, provides the classic example of this problem. Nigeria has over 250 different ethnic groups, almost all of whom speak their own individual languages. The three dominant groups, the Hausa, Yoruba, and Ibo, have been rivals for centuries. Until the colonial period, Nigeria's ethnic groups lived independently, occasionally warring with their neighbors. The British forced all of them to combine under one national government, but their distrust of each other continues.

In some cases ethnic competition exists because one or two smaller groups monopolize rich mineral resources, such as oil along the coast of Nigeria or diamonds in Sierra Leone. In other cases ethnic tension is related to the regional split between the north and the south, which is especially critical in Nigeria. Northern parts of these nations tend to have less potential for economic wealth than the southern regions. This leads to intense rivalries over how tax money and development projects should be distributed.

In addition to economics, the northern areas of countries such as Nigeria, Ghana, Ivory Coast, Benin, and Togo tend to be dominated by Muslims, who are often distrustful of their southern non-Muslim neighbors. Tensions between Muslims and non-Muslims, mixed with the anxiety from unequal economic development, often erupts into riots and, in extreme cases, civil war.

Leadership for the Future

Since independence, leaders in some West African countries have exploited these tensions and divisions. Sometimes government officials steal money intended for social projects such as schools and hospitals. In Nigeria, for example, the last military ruler became a billionaire by controlling oil rig and pipeline construction and oil and gas sales, money that was supposed to go to national development programs.

Frequently, governments are overthrown by coup d'états, or forceful oustings, usually led by a military general. Some coup leaders, such as Ghana's Jerry

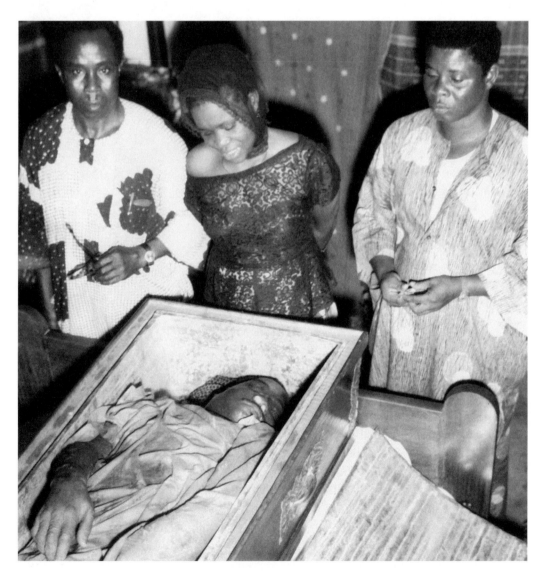

Long-standing conflicts between Nigerian ethnic groups erupted in a bloody civil war in 1967.

Rawlings, manage to prepare their nations for democratic elections. But just as frequently, coup leaders are overthrown by rivals for power in new coups.

Often the widespread violence that accompanies the coups expands into civil wars, which stunt a nation's potential for growth. Nigeria, Liberia, and Sierra Leone are three of the more tragic examples. In recent years Sierra Leone was ranked by the U.S. State Department as the most dangerous nation in the world because of its extended civil war. The conflict wrecked the entire educational system. Instead of attending school, armed eleven- and twelve-year-old boys rampaged through villages slaughtering or maiming everyone in their path.

All hope for a more peaceful future is not lost, however. West African nations also have experience with democracy. In fact, the trend since the early 1990s has been toward freer elections. All West African leaders claim that some form of democratic society is necessary for the long-term growth of their national economies.

The real problem lies in finding a way to blend a stable federal government with strong state and local governments. The best leaders have the ability to connect diverse groups of people under a common

Elected in 1999, Nigerian president Olusegun Obasanjo is working to rebuild and diversify the nation's economy.

national goal, and West Africa is lucky to have several strong leaders who are leading their nations toward full democracy.

The most notable leader today is Nigerian president Olusegun Obasanjo. Winning in freely contested elections in

Sam Jonah

One of Ghanaian president Jerry Rawlings's policies is to recruit talent from inside his country to lead businesses. To head the important Ashanti mining corporation, Rawlings chose Sam Jonah, an unknown but eager worker. Reporters Johanna McGeary and Marguerite Michaels describe Sam Jonah's rise in a March 30, 1998, *Time* magazine feature.

"Jonah was the seventh child of 10; he grew up in Obuasi, site of Ashanti's richest gold mine. Jonah went down into the mine while awaiting a promised scholarship from Ashanti. 'It was character forging,' he says. 'I know about teamwork, and I can still speak the mining slang.' After study at University of Exeter's Camborne School of Mines, he returned to Obuasi, starting as a shift boss deep in the pits and working his way up—and out—the first black man to climb the ranks.

Rawlings chose Jonah in 1982 as deputy managing director of Ashanti, then owned 55% by the government and 45% by London's Lonrho Corp. 'I didn't know him,' says Jonah. 'He just reached out for the highest-ranking Ghanaian.' In 1986 Jonah rose to the top job, becoming, according to him, the only black African CEO of a multinational company. 'The obstacle to there being more like me on this continent relates to one thing,' says Jonah. 'Ownership. If Rawlings had not taken a personal interest in the mining sector, the level of prejudice would have kept me underground forever. I still tell my Ghanaians,' he adds, 'Don't accept no!'"

Under Jonah, Ghana has learned the art, which is rare in Africa, of managing its natural resources effectively. Ashanti has led the country's gold production to record highs. Floating public shares on the New York Stock Exchange in 1994, the government sold off 30 percent of its interest. Then Jonah went shopping, acquiring mining interests and prospecting rights in fifteen other African states. Instead of confirming that any multinational company involving foreign owners will only exploit African labor and steal Africa's natural resources for the benefit of shareholders overseas, Rawlings and Jonah have turned Ashanti into a model for made-in-Africa industrialization.

Ghanaian president Jerry Rawlings, who has put talented countrymen like Sam Jonah in top industrial posts, visited the United States in 1999.

1999, Obasanjo is carefully guiding his nation out of a long period of economic depression caused by corrupt military governments. Besides trying to restore people's trust in government, he has promoted initiatives to diversify the Nigerian economy. For farmers, he has offered financial incentives to expand irrigation. He has also embarked on a campaign to turn over more of the economy to private ownership.

Another leader overseeing his nation's progress is Ghana's Jerry Rawlings. Al-though much smaller than Nigeria, Ghana possesses a variety of resources that will enable the people to build a strong country. After taking power in a military coup in 1981, Rawlings slowly moved his country toward a free and diversified economy. In 1992 he defeated several candidates in an open election and became president. During his second term, he launched Vision 2020, a plan to expand the national economy so that Ghana will have a middle-class population by 2020.

Kwame Nkrumah of Ghana, left, an influential proponent of African unity in the 1950s, greets leaders from Ceylon.

The key to Rawlings's success is finding and encouraging Ghanaian citizens to invest their talents and money in the nation's economy instead of depending on foreign sources.

African Unity and Cooperation

In the 1950s Ghana's Kwame Nkrumah jumped into the spotlight with his revolutionary views about African unity. Only by pooling the continent's resources and population under a single government, he argued, could Africa become a powerful influence in world affairs. Others, like Nigeria's Nnamdi Azikiwe, believed that regional and continental unity was possible only after each country built its own firm economic and political foundation.

In May 1963 thirty nations formed the Organization of African Unity (OAU). Their goals were to eliminate colonialism, support peace among member states, assist economic development, promote human rights, and protect the environment. Today fifty-three nations are members. One of the OAU's successes involved pressuring nations around the world to stop trade and cooperation with South Africa until that country eliminated its governmental policy of racial discrimination and permitted free elections.

Regional organizations have become just as influential as the OAU. In 1975 West African countries formed the West African Economic and Monetary Union. By 1993 sixteen West African countries

belonged to the union. Their major goals include creating a common tariff for trade, allowing people to travel freely throughout the region, modernizing highways and telecommunications, halting desertification, improving rural water systems, and cooperating on national economic planning. A branch of the union, the West African Peacekeeping Force, has been called on to intervene in civil wars.

The union's success has encouraged West Africans to form other private regional groups, including a privately owned regional commercial bank, the Federation of West African Manufacturers Associations, the Federation of West African Chambers of Commerce, the West African Journalists Association, the West African Youth Union, the West African Women's Association, and the West African Road Transporters Union.

West Africa's Future

During the twentieth century, European educations and new technologies revolutionized Africans' worldview. From the local through national levels, West Africans began shedding their traditional customs. Governments felt the pressure to raise living standards immediately. Today world leaders continue to criticize West Africa for its lack of democracy, but a few of the smaller nations have made progress, notably Ghana and Senegal. It takes time to adapt to such rapid change, however.

Most of these nations have yet to find a solution to the intense ethnic rivalries

Kofi Annan and His Dream of Peacekeeping

Ghana's Kofi Annan stepped into the world spotlight in December 1997 when he accepted the four-year position as the seventh secretary-general of the United Nations (UN). He has become one of the most respected individuals in the world for his calm manner of handling crises. In *Time*'s cover feature on September 4, 2000, journalist Joshua Cooper Ramo writes, "In dangerous situations—the kind that would have most of us tingling with a little bit of healthy fear—Annan becomes calmer, aides say."

The appointment culminated a life-long career with the international organization. Annan's major contribution to world peace is his idea of humanitarian intervention, an extension of the UN's role in promoting peace and improving living standards around the globe. On a PBS interview for *NewsHour* in October 1999, Annan explained his views.

"The UN was set up after World War II, and at that point we were more concerned about interstate warfare. Today most of the wars we are concerned about are intrastate. On how we deal with interstate warfare there was a consensus and the consensus had been maintained up till now, but we are living in a new era where the conflicts are internal, and yet, we have not come up with a new consensus as to . . . how we define the common interest, who defines the common interest, how we defend the common interest, when we intervene, and when we do not."

He went on to explain that intervention did not have to mean sending in military troops. "The establishment of the two [war crimes] tribunals for Rwanda and the former Yugoslavia is a deterrent," he pointed out. "The attempts by the international community to establish an international criminal court will be a deterrent, and really send a message out to those who would commit these heinous crimes that you have nowhere to hide, you will be made accountable."

Known for keeping a cool head in hot situations, Kofi Annan of Ghana was named secretary general of the UN in 1997.

within their own boundaries. West African leaders see a long transitional period ahead that contradicts outside pressure for immediate democracy. For the next fifty years or more, they will be concentrating on building unity within their countries. It will be a difficult task.

Carrying half of the region's population, Nigeria is in the spotlight. However, it forever seems to totter on the brink of civil war between its northern and southern regions. For most of its history as an independent nation, Nigeria has been controlled by military rulers, in part because of the ethnic and regional instability. With the weight of West Africa on its shoulders, Nigeria staggers into the twenty-first century still searching for its own clear path to a solid national unity. A stable Nigeria, with its enormous economic potential, would stand tall as a model and leader for the entire continent, not just for West Africa.

Notes

Chapter 2: Kingdoms of the Western Sudan

1. Quoted in Basil Davidson, *A History of West Africa to the Nineteenth Century*. Garden City, NJ: Doubleday, 1966, p. 43.

2. E. W. Bovill, *The Golden Trade of the Moors*. London: Oxford University Press, 1963, p. 82.

3. Patricia and Fredrick McKissack, *The Royal Kingdoms of Ghana, Mali, and Songhay: Life in Medieval Africa*. New York: Henry Holt, 1995, p. 47.

4. Lavinia Dobler and William A. Brown, *Great Rulers of the African Past*. Garden City, NJ: Zenith Books/Doubleday, 1965, p. 35.

5. Quoted in McKissack, *The Royal Kingdoms of Ghana, Mali, and Songhay*, p. 102.

6. Quoted in McKissack, *The Royal Kingdoms of Ghana, Mali, and Songhay*, p. 105.

7. Quoted in J. Spencer Trimingham, *A History of Islam in West Africa*. London: Oxford University Press, 1963, p. 145.

8. Quoted in J. F. Ade Ajayi and Ian Espie, eds., *A Thousand Years of West African History: A Handbook for Teachers and Students*. Ibadan, Nigeria: Ibadan University Press, 1965, p. 266.

9. Thomas Hodgkin, "Uthman dan Fodio," *Nigeria 1960*. 1960, p. 80.

Chapter 3: The Forest Kingdoms

10. Quoted in Thomas Hodgkin, ed., *Nigerian Perspectives: An Historical Anthology*. London: Oxford University Press, 1960, p. 122.

11. Ajayi and Espie, *A Thousand Years of West African History*, p. 255.

12. Quoted in Hodgkin, *Nigerian Perspectives*, p. 149.

13. Quoted in Hodgkin, *Nigerian Perspectives*, p. 151.

14. Quoted in Ajayi and Espie, *A Thousand Years of West African History*, p. 172.

15. Quoted in Ajayi and Espie, *A Thousand Years of West African History*, p. 309.

16. Quoted in Davidson, *A History of West Africa*, p. 233.

Chapter 4: From Colonialism to Independence

17. Quoted in Basil Davidson, *The African Slave Trade: Precolonial History, 1450–1850*. Boston: Little, Brown, 1961, p. 42.

18. Quoted in Davidson, *The African Slave Trade*, p. 20.

19. Quoted in Davidson, *A History of West Africa*, p. 227.

20. Quoted in Hodgkin, *Nigerian Perspectives*, p. 296.

21. Quoted in Hodgkin, *Nigerian Perspectives*, p. 306.

Chapter 5: Family and Community

22. Quoted in Richard Olaniyan, ed., *African History and Culture*. Ikeja, Nigeria: Longman, 1982, p. 141.

23. John S. Mbiti, *African Religions and Philosophy*. Garden City, NJ: Anchor Books, 1970, pp. 175–176.

24. Camara Laye, *The Dark Child*. New York: Farrar, Straus, and Giroux, 1954, pp. 94, 96.

25. Laye, *The Dark Child*, p. 100.

26. Laye, *The Dark Child*, p. 128.

27. Sobonfu and Malidoma Some, "From Whence We Came," *Essence*, December 1999, p. 86.

28. Wole Soyinka, *Ake: The Years of Childhood*. New York: Vintage International, 1989, p. 79.

29. Quoted in Johanna McGeary and Marguerite Michaels, "Africa Rising," *Time,* March 30, 1998. www.time.com/time/magazine/1998/dom/980330/cover5.html.

Chapter 6: Religion

30. Innocent Onyewuenyi, "Reincarnation: An Impossible Concept in the Framework of African Ontology," *African Traditional Religion*. http://isizoh.net/afrel/atr-reincarnation.htm.

31. Mbiti, *African Religions and Philosophy*, p. 320.

32. Quoted in Hodgkin, *Nigerian Perspectives*, p. 100.

33. Quoted in Jacob K. Olupona, ed., *African Traditional Religions in Contemporary Societies*. New York: Paragon House, 1991, p. 52.

34. Yushau Sodiq, letter to author, July 3, 2000.

Chapter 7: The Arts

35. Quoted in Roger D. Abrahams, *African Folktales: Traditional Stories of the Black World*. New York: Pantheon, 1983, p. 9.

36. Frank Willett, *African Art: An Introduction*. New York: Praeger, 1971, p. 112.

37. Ayo Bankole, Judith Bush, and Sadek H. Samaan, "The Yoruba Master Drummer," *Africa Arts,* Winter 1975, p. 48.

38. Bankole, Bush, and Samaan, "The Yoruba Master Drummer," p. 50.

39. David Gilden, "The Ngoni," *Cora Connection*. www.coraconnection.com/pages/ngoni.html.

40. Quoted in "Ghana." www.africaonline.com/AfricaOnline/music/Ghana.html.

41. Quoted in Melanie McGee, "Golden Voice: Mali's Salif Keita Turns Tragedy into Triumph." www.mountainx.com/ae/1999/0120keita.html.

42. Abrahams, *African Folktales*, p. 13.

Chapter 8: The Future of West Africa

43. Stephen Buckley, "Families of Abidjan: Families' Ties Can Get Knotty," *Washington Post*, 1997.www.washingtonpost.com/wp-srv/inatl/longterm/africanlives/abidjan/abidjan.htm.

44. Quoted in McGeary and Michaels, "Africa Rising."

For Further Reading

Books

Roger D. Abrahams, *African Folktales: Traditional Stories of the Black World*. New York: Pantheon, 1983. This is an excellent source for African lore. It includes stories from the traditional trickster to fairy tales, stories about social relations and dilemma tales, and stories of heroes and royalty and the gods and goddesses. Each unit is introduced with an excellent essay that ties in African stories with stories from around the world.

Lavinia Dobler and William A. Brown, *Great Rulers of the African Past*. Garden City, NJ: Zenith Books/Doubleday, 1965. This is an excellent introduction to the famous rulers of African kingdoms, covering the accomplishments and character of Mansa Mūsā of Mali, Sunni Ali Ber and Askia Muhammad of Songhai, Affonso I of Kongo, and King Idris Alooma of Bornu. It includes some detail of daily life in their kingdoms.

The Heritage Library of African Peoples. New York: Rosen, 1996. This series covers dozens of ethnic groups throughout Africa. Each volume describes the history and culture of a different ethnic group, providing valuable details.

Camara Laye, *The Dark Child*. New York: Farrar, Straus, and Giroux, 1954. Laye's autobiography is simple but respectful of traditional African beliefs as well as Islamic influences. He writes about his parents, initiation to manhood, and courting his girlfriend while attending school. In the end, like so many talented young Africans, Laye decided to leave his country for several years to attend school overseas.

Patricia and Fredrick McKissack, *The Royal Kingdoms of Ghana, Mali, and Songhay: Life in Medieval Africa*. New York: Henry Holt, 1995. This outstanding introduction to the ancient kingdoms of Ghana, Mali, and Songhai goes into vivid detail about the life and culture of the people, including discussions of work, religion, and trade. It gives good profiles of the major leaders of Mali and Songhai and discussions of Timbuktu, Gao, and Djenné.

John Owhonda, *Nigeria: A Nation of Many People*. Parsippany, NJ: Dillon, 1998. This book is an excellent introduction to Nigeria, its people, and its culture. Separate chapters are included on education, arts and entertainment, oral traditions, and Nigerians living in the United States.

Geoffrey Parrinder, *African Mythology*. New York: Peter Bedrick Books, 1987. An excellent discussion of African legends, from the stories of creation and first ancestors, the spirit world, and secret societies to animal fables and many other topics. There are dozens of colorful photos of art pieces illustrating the discussions.

Margaret Shinnie, *Ancient African Kingdoms*. New York: New American Library, 1965. This introduction to African kingdoms covers early Africa, from the northeastern kingdom of Kush to the southern kingdom of Zimbabwe, and many in between. It includes discussions of Ghana, Mali, Songhai, Kanem-Bornu, and the forest states of Benin and Ashanti.

Internet Sources

University of Pennsylvania African Studies Website (www.sas. upenn.edu/African_Studies/Home_Page/AFR_GIDE.html) This site contains extensive sources, especially relating to specific country sites. These include links to the "K–12 Electronic Guide for African Resources on the Internet," which summarizes material available on the university's website, and *Africa Access*, an electronic review evaluating children's materials on Africa.

Yale–New Haven Teachers Institute Resource on African Masks (www.yale.edu/ynhti/curriculum/units/1985/6/85.06.06.x.html) This site is an excellent source of information on masks in West Africa, including their uses, how they are carved, and their connections with secret societies. "The Mask—a West African Ceremonial Object" is an essay and lesson plan by Sharon L. Mullen, a middle-school teacher who uses the Kpelie face mask of the Senufo ethnic group from Ivory Coast. The website also allows students to choose and make their own masks.

Works Consulted

Books

Chinua Achebe, *Things Fall Apart*. Portsmouth, NH: Heinemann, 1996. This was the first published novel in the acclaimed African Writers series, setting the standard for all modern African fiction. With guidance, the novel is an excellent source for introducing the traditional culture of Nigeria's Ibo people.

J. F. Ade Ajayi and Ian Espie, eds., *A Thousand Years of West African History: A Handbook for Teachers and Students*. Ibadan, Nigeria: Ibadan University Press, 1965. Generated by a workshop at the University of Ibadan, Nigeria, this book looks at African history through the views of Africans instead of Europeans. Sections cover West African history from the ancient kingdom of Ghana to European colonialism. It includes articles by J. F. Ade Ajayi, "West African States at the Beginning of the Nineteenth Century," I. A. Akinjogbin, "Dahomey and Yoruba in the Nineteenth Century," A. Adu Boahen, "Asante and Fante, A.D. 1000–1800," and J. O. Hunwick, "The Nineteenth Century Jihads."

E. W. Bovill, *The Golden Trade of the Moors*. London: Oxford University Press, 1963. This book details the contact between North Africa and the western Sudan. It utilizes eyewitness sources as well as Bovill's background in the field of trans-Saharan trade.

Basil Davidson, *The African Slave Trade: Precolonial History, 1450–1850*. Boston: Little, Brown, 1961. One of the major studies of the slave trade. This book looks at the facts, discusses how the trade was carried out, who was involved throughout Africa, and the reaction of Africans to the abolition movement.

———, *A History of West Africa to the Nineteenth Century*. Garden City, NJ: Doubleday, 1966. This is perhaps the major source for learning about the life and history of West Africa up to the 1800s. It includes the major kingdoms, from the western Sudan to the Guinea coast, and the cultural and social life of the people.

Thomas Hodgkin, ed., *Nigerian Perspectives: An Historical Anthology*. London: Oxford University Press, 1960. This includes excerpts from participants in Nigeria's history, from European explorers and missionaries to Nigerians such as Uthman dan Fodio. It also has Nigerian praise songs and parts of the famous *Kano Chronicle*. It includes articles by Count C. N. de Cardi, "King Ja-Ja of Opobo," and Mary Kingsley, "The Niger Delta at the End of the Century."

G. I. Jones, *The Trading States of the Oil Rivers: A Study of Political Development in Eastern Nigeria*. London: Oxford University Press, 1963. This study offers great detail of the nineteenth-century Niger Delta society. Jones explains the oral traditions of the people, their economic and political "canoe house" system, the competitiveness of the slave trade, and the shift in trade to palm oil. It has extensive genealogy tables, lists of kings, and maps.

John S. Mbiti, *African Religions and Philosophy*. Garden City, NJ: Anchor Books, 1970. Once considered the foremost expert on African religions, Mbiti begins with Africans' concept of time and progresses through their beliefs in a creator god, the spirits and ancestors, ethnic and community cohesion, rituals, death, magic, and mystical power. The book concludes with chapters on the impact of Christianity and Islam on Africa and Africans' search for identity in the late twentieth century.

Richard Olaniyan, ed., *African History and Culture*. Ikeja, Nigeria: Longman, 1982. This anthology has fourteen essays on African culture, covering everything from art and music to religion and politics. The essay by John S. Mbiti, "African Views of the Universe," explains Africans' belief in a creator, the nature of the creator's universe, and how humans are really the center of the universe.

Roland Oliver and J. D. Fage, *A Short History of Africa*. 5th ed. Middlesex, England: Penguin, 1986. This book may be short, but it covers chronologically an enormous amount of detail on the history of the entire continent; an excellent source.

Jacob K. Olupona, ed., *African Traditional Religions in Contemporary Societies*. New York: Paragon House, 1991. An anthology with scholarly essays on the status of religion in modern Africa.

It covers areas such as the talking drum, women in traditional African religions, the Yoruba divinity Sango (or Shango), Islam and Christianity and their impact on traditional religions, and new religious movements. Wande Abimbola's essay "The Place of African Traditional Religion in Contemporary Africa: The Yoruba Example" explains his views about how the Yoruba assimilate other religions into their belief system.

Wole Soyinka, *Ake: The Years of Childhood.* New York: Vintage International, 1989. A Nobel Prize winner for literature, Soyinka describes his boyhood in Abeokuta, Nigeria. An excellent source for learning about the daily life of a young Nigerian between 1934 and 1945.

J. Spencer Trimingham, *A History of Islam in West Africa.* London: Oxford University Press, 1963. This extremely detailed account is still the basic source for studying Islam's spread throughout West Africa. It includes extensive quotes and notes.

West Africa. Melbourne, Australia: Lonely Planet Publications, 1999. Although for tourists, this book contains dozens of excellent capsule descriptions of West African culture, including an excellent introduction to modern popular music and the flora and fauna. A good beginning for anyone wanting a general overview.

Frank Willett, *African Art: An Introduction.* New York: Praeger, 1971. One of the major experts in African art, Willett introduces African culture, moves on to the development of African art, covers in separate chapters African architecture and sculpture, and then concludes with a chapter on modern African art.

Periodicals

Ayo Bankole, Judith Bush, and Sadek H. Samaan, "The Yoruba Master Drummer," *Africa Arts*, Winter 1975.

Thomas Hodgkin, "Uthman dan Fodio," *Nigeria 1960*, 1960.

Roderic Knight, "Mandinka Drumming," *Africa Arts*, Summer 1974.

Z. K. Oloruntoba, Gretchen Dihoff, and Michael W. Peplow, "A Dream of King Marapaka," *African Arts*, Summer 1970.

James A. Perry, "African Roots of African-American Culture," *Black Collegian*, October 1998.

Joshua Cooper Ramo, "The Five Virtues of Kofi Annan," *Time*, September 2000.

Sandra Rattley-Lewis, "Family Reunion: Coming Home to Ghana," *Essence,* April 1998.

Sobonfu and Malidoma Some, "From Whence We Came," *Essence*, December 1999.

Robert Farris Thompson, "An Aesthetic of the Cool," *African Arts*, Autumn 1973.

Cootje Van Oven, "Music of Sierra Leone," *African Arts*, Summer 1970.

Internet Sources

"Background to Ashanti." www.gla.ac.uk/~gkea04/ashanti.html.

Stephen Buckley, "Families of Abidjan: Families' Ties Can Get Knotty," *Washington Post*, 1997. www.washingtonpost.com/wp-srv/inatl/longterm/africanlives/abidjan/abidjan.htm.

"Celebration of History: Gambia Hosts Roots Festival for Africa's Children," *Final Call Online,* April 2, 1997. www.hartford-hwp.com/archives/34/017.html.

Michael Conner, "Welcome to Cutting to the Essence, Shaping for the Fire." www.fa.indiana.edu/~conner/africart/home.html.

"Ghana." www.africaonline.com/AfricaOnline/music/Ghana.html.

David Gilden, "The Ngoni," Cora Connection. www.coraconnection.com/pages/ngoni.html.

Mitsuru Hamamoto, "Africa's Best-Known Reggae Star," *Drum*, October 1993. www.alphablondy.org/life.html.

Interview with Kofi Annan, *On Line NewsHour*, October 18, 1999. www.pbs.org/newshour/bb/international/july-dec99/annan_10–18.html.

Jen Kriesel, Brent Janaky, and Brian Herro, "The Drum Language." http://gbms01.uwgb.edu/~galta/mrr/ashanti/drum.htm.

San Kwadjovie, "Masks of Africa," *Legacy,* Winter 1998–1999. www.ngilegacy.com/pdf/wintertext.pdf.

Maria McCloy, "Mali's Songbird." www.mg.co.za/mg/art/reviews/97sep/11sep-women1.html.

Johanna McGeary and Marguerite Michaels, "Africa Rising," *Time*, March 30, 1998. www.time.com/time/magazine/1998/dom/980330/cover5.html.

Melanie McGee, "Golden Voice: Mali's Salif Keita Turns Tragedy into Triumph." www.mountainx.com/ae/1999/0120keita.html.

Innocent Onyewuenyi, "Reincarnation: An Impossible Concept in the Framework of African Ontology," *African Traditional Religion*. http://isizoh.net/afrel/atr-reincarnation.htm.

Robert Palmer, "Griots of West Africa, an Introduction Essay." *Griots of West Africa and Beyond*, 1997. www.uni-paderborn.de/~pg/kunda.html.

Mike Thomas, "Babatunde Olatunji: Delivering the Cure," *Salon*, January 8, 2000. www.salon.com/people/feature/2000/01/08/olatunji/index1.html.

Index

Picture Credits

Cover photo: © Jim Zuckerman/Corbis
© Paul Almasy/Corbis, 83, 85
© Tiziana and Gianni Baldizzone/Corbis, 17
Des Bartlett, Photo Researchers, Inc., NYC, 16
© Bettmann/Corbis, 44
© Contemporary African Art Collection Limited/Corbis, 48, 69
Culver Pictures, Inc., 23, 34, 39, 66
© Owen Franken/Corbis, 14, 87
© Marc Garanger/Corbis, 60
© Kerstin Geier, Gallo Images/Corbis, 53
© George Gerster/Photo Researchers, Inc., NYC, 54
F. B. Grunzweig/Photo Researchers, Inc., NYC, 72
© Chester Higgins Jr./Photo Researchers, Inc., NYC, 56
Hulton Getty Collection/Archive Photos, 45, 80, 89, 92
© Jacques Jangoux/Photo Researchers, Inc., NYC, 12
© Wolfgang Kaehler/Corbis, 71
Kean Collection/Archive Photos, 25
© Daniel Laine/Corbis, 32
© Charles and Josette Lenars/Corbis, 70
Library of Congress, 40
North Wind Picture Archives, 21, 36, 38
© Neal Preston/Corbis, 77
© Diane Rawson/Photo Researchers, Inc., NYC, 28
Reuters/Larry Downing/Archive Photos, 91
Reuters/Corinne Dufka/Archive Photos, 90
Reuters/Pierre Virot/Archive Photos, 94
© Fulvio Roiter/Corbis, 74
© Rykoff Collection/Corbis, 64
Martha Schierholz, 9, 10, 30
© Adam G. Sylvester/Photo Researchers, Inc., 51
© Nick Wheeler/Corbis, 19, 62

About the Author

Tony Zurlo taught in Nigeria with the Peace Corps and at a teacher's university in China. He lives in Arlington, Texas, with his wife, an artist/educator from China. His publications include the books *Japan: Superpower of the Pacific* and *China: The Dragon Awakes*. He is currently working on a book about Hong Kong. His poetry, fiction, reviews, and essays have appeared in over sixty literary magazines and newspapers.